Discarded

Veatrice Chapin

ISBN   978-1-949309-63-8

Sierra Sunset Publishing

Acknowledgments

My Special Thanks To:

- Members of the Sacramento Suburban Writers' Club Critique Group, authors and writers Ron, Mary Lou, Cathy, Karen, and Tammy for critiquing page by page and encouraging with positive and sometimes painful criticism that resulted in this book.

- My Beta Readers Paul, Ann, Barbara, and Jan for giving me the final "go."

- My ever-patient family and friends who have encouraged me to publish.

- Friend Patti and sister-in-law Lisa for believing in me, along with my daughter Jennifer who named my book.

I take courage from their love and friendship.

1

I stand on the towering stone walls of the prison overlooking the cove where another ship has just arrived from England to bring their worst to this dry, dreadful land. England has a respectable reputation to uphold, and we don't fit. Year after year, massive wooden ships sail far across the vast ocean waters to rid them of this plight, and the Australian prisons are their answer.

I can't help but wonder why our Queen has people she thinks of as worthless. There's no thought to how the prisoners are treated or what happens to them. My heart goes out to them, for I know their lives have become a living hell.

Watching the prisoners being unloaded brings back hurtful memories from a time when, I too, made that brutal voyage. Bound in shackles and chains down deep in the belly of a hellish ship, I was forced to stay in unholy conditions like an animal. The slats on the floor did little to keep me from the filth, vomit, and human waste. The only thing I could do was pray that somehow I would live. Some on board didn't survive, but like me, those who did, our lives were forever changed.

Who am I, and why am I standing on the wall of this godless place? My name is Adeleen. At the young age of nine, I killed a man by cracking his skull with a heavy hammer. He was a well-known, wealthy aristocrat, and one of England's upper class. It wasn't until I was in jail that I learned I was the bastard child of that man. My being so young it was hard for me to understand what I did, or why things happen the way they did.

His family demanded, even though I was a child, that I have a sentence of execution for killing him. Instead, the court magistrate chose to be merciful and send me to Australia to live out a life sentence with no hope of ever leaving.

I didn't know much about life when I came here, but the huge hurt and an enormous will to survive are what have helped me to endure my cruel life sentence.

2

London, 1859

Hearing a buggy pull up outside our little house, my mum, older brother Benjamin and I go to peek out the window. It's the tall man with the black hat, along with two other men. He never brings anyone with him to our house when he comes to see my mum. Why this time?

I look at her, waiting to see her usual nod that means for my brother and me to be off to the neighbors. But this time it's different — she doesn't nod. Instead, I see fear on her face as she yells, "Hide children, and don't let them catch you, no matter what!"

With no time to get out of the house, or ask why, I run to hide behind the curtains, while my brother crouches behind a big chair. Peeking through the curtains, I watch as my mum opens the door. The two men push their way into our house, one grabbing her by the hair, then both men drag her outside, throwing her in the dirt at the tall man's feet.

Benjamin bolts from behind the chair and runs out the door after them, trying his best to help her. Kicking and hitting the men, he struggles trying to keep them away from her.

As I watch in horror through the slits in the curtains, I hear my mum's screams. Afraid, I back up even further behind the curtains trying to hide. Putting my hands over my ears, I close my eyes, hoping they won't see me. I feel the floor under my feet moving as someone enters the house again. My heart pounds from fright, but I stay quiet with my eyes shut tight, and holding my breath.

I can still hear Benjamin outside yelling, but I stand still. Then the curtain yanks back. I let out a scream and start to run as one of the men reaches for me.

"Come here!" he yells, grabbing hold of my hair and dragging me kicking and screaming across the floor. I turn and sink my teeth into his leg as hard as I can. With a tight grip on me he shakes me, and yells for me to stop.

Suddenly, my brother races back in through the doorway, and jumps on the man's back, biting his ear. It's then I bite the man's arm causing him to let me go so I can run. Little children can't fight, but we surely can bite.

The man pulls Benjamin away, knocking him to the floor. I see an open window across the room, so I run and jump through it, just as the man reaches out and grabs the bow on the back of my dress. It rips away, but it doesn't matter, I'm already out the window and running as fast as my legs can take me.

Rushing down the street into the bitter cold night, I leave Benjamin and my mum behind. It's scary for a nine-year-old to be out in the dark. But, I run for what seems like forever until I can't run anymore. It's freezing, and I'm getting tired, so I stop. Looking around for a place to feel safe, I see three giant wooden boxes beside an old tool shed and crawl into a space behind them to hide. Still afraid, I sit wrapping my arms tightly around my knees, and stay there all night in the damp cold too terrified to go home. I don't understand what is happening, or why they want to hurt my mum!

Shaking and worried, I begin to cry. I don't know where Benjamin is, or if he saved Mum from those bad men. For a moment I get brave, making fists with both my hands. *I'll hit anyone who tries to grab me! I'll fight them!* Then I start sobbing, putting my forehead on my knees as tears flow down my cheeks. Shivering from the cold, I curl up trying to stay warm throughout the night. I can't control my crying, and softly whisper, "Mummy. Mummy. Why did you tell me to hide?"

Sometime in the night I must have fallen asleep. When I wake the next morning, I notice the door on the nearby shed is ajar. Looking around to make sure no one is watching, I hurry over and open it wider to peek inside. Thinking it might be a safer place for me to hide,

I step in and carefully latch the door behind me. I'm still frightened and confused, I'm hoping my mum and Benjamin will come and find me.

With the bright sunlight shining in through an open window at the back of the shed, I look around at all the tools. Wanting to protect myself, I grab something. Upset and hungry, I stay there through the morning with a tight grip on a hammer. Again I become sleepy, so I lie down to nap.

Noise outside awakens me. Terrified, I move into a corner. Suddenly the door opens. It's one of those men from the house.

"She's in here," he yells, then closes the door again.

Screaming, I wet myself. Crying loudly, I bury my face in my hands not understanding what's happening. I hear footsteps and talking. Then, nothing. Sitting still, I try to listen to what's happening outside. It stays quiet for what seems like a long time.

Soon I hear horses and wheels approaching on the cobblestone road. Suddenly, the latch lifts on the door, and it slowly opens. A figure of a tall man steps inside, closing the door behind. It's him, the man my mum told me to hide from. I stare at him, and he at me. Then the corner of his mouth smiles this ugly sick smile as he reaches for me...he doesn't see my hammer.

❧❧❧❧❧

It all happens so fast. I'm taken to a police station and given over to a bobby dressed in a tidy black jacket with gold buttons. He tells me to wait on the bench beside others who are in shackles. I look at the smelly, ragged man next to me and make a putrid face. He opens his eyes wide and frightens me.

I begin to cry and repeatedly call out for my mum, but the bobbies' give me their stupid smile and say, "Be quiet, little girl." Then they reassure me they will try to find her, but I think they're lying.

"Come with me, young lady," one of the bobbies says as he grabs me by my arm and leads me towards a big courtroom. "You have to see the Magistrate now, so come along and shut your mouth."

The Magistrate is a scary man who sits up high behind a big desk and is wearing a silly-looking white wig on his head. He has a grumpy look on his face as he stares down at me. I hear him ask the man beside me questions about what I did.

"Your Worship, this young girl hit her father with a hammer, killing him. His family is here demanding something to be done to her for this devastating, heinous crime."

What? Confused, I stare at the man. I don't have a father...do I? My mum never said that. Upset, I look around at all the people in the courtroom, hoping to see my mum or Benjamin. They can tell the scary Magistrate that she told me to run and hide. I don't know the man I hit. I only hit him once when he grabbed me.

I'm startled when the gavel slams down. Looking back at the Magistrate, I hear his decision..."Transportation!" I'm to be punished for the terrible wrong I've done.

The Magistrate says because I'm so young, it's best if I'm kept in the London jail until the age of twelve before sending me away.

"Take her out!" slamming his gavel again.

One of the bobbies takes me down several long, dimly lit hallways farther away from the courtroom. I become fearful and panic, trying to pull away from his grip, but he quickly yanks my arm.

With tears running down my cheeks, I cry out, "Where are you taking me? I want to go home! I want my mummy!"

"No...you're going to live with us now, so quit yer sniveling." Grabbing me by the nape of my neck he drags me.

Unlocking a big iron door, we move into a large, smelly room that has a lot of bars on both sides. As we walk into the room, I notice people sitting on beds. Most of them stand up and put their arms out through the bars to watch us as we come in. Everyone is staring at me. I shudder at their terrifying faces. Crying, and stomping my feet, I bury my face in the bobby's topcoat.

He grabs me tighter, and pushes me towards one of the locked doors. Putting in a big key, he turns it, and I hear the lock clank open. Two ragged-looking women step forward as he shoves me into their cell. As soon as he let go, I run for one of the beds. The blankets are messy and dirty.

"Oh no, you don't," pointing for me to go to a bed in the corner. "Get over there," says a mean lady with a black eye.

"Well, well, what do we have here, a little red-head Irish brat," says the other lady who has dirty grey hair.

Too afraid to say anything, I just frown. I want to tell them, my mummy is Irish and me and my brother we got red hair just like hers, but my mouth is frozen shut with fear.

"You don't wet the bed, do you, child? Cause we don't want no bed wetter in here."

Shaking my head no, I still don't say a word. I don't tell them I wet myself in the shed.

"Don't you worry little one, we won't let anything happen to you," says the lady with the black eye glaring at the bobby as if to say move on. He doesn't say anything either but steps back and locks the bar door behind him.

So, for the next three years, I learn that I shouldn't have done what I did to the man they said was my father. Neither my mum nor Benjamin ever comes to find me. What's happened to them?

One day I find myself being loaded onto one of those giant transport ships to spend the rest of my life far away from home. England doesn't want me, and I don't understand why. I don't think I'm bad, but they send me there anyway. Where are they taking me? Fremantle, Western Australia. Known as England's harshest prison, the prison they call, "The Establishment."

3

1862

The voyage is long and seems to never end. The motion of the ship changes daily. At times it rolls gently on the water, then at any moment will violently toss in a storm. Hour after hour the motion never stops, causing me to get sick.

Looking around I feel sad. Some prisoners become weak from vomiting and the lack of water. They soon die. Daily the crew comes below to look for the dead to toss overboard. Will I live? Do I even want to?

The cruelty from the crew never stops. If anyone tries to speak, they push them aside or hit them with their clubs, yelling for them to sit down and shut up. We mean nothing to them.

There are men and women prisoners on board. Some prisoners will be allowed to return to England after they serve their sentence. Others, like me, will have to live out the rest of our lives at the vile living hell on earth, the prison.

Suddenly, the ship shakes with a loud noise as the anchor drops, slowing it to a stop. There's an eerie silence as we stare at one another. I've heard about this place, but only horror stories that pave the way to my future.

The guards come below, unlocking the chains that have bound us for months.

"Stand up!" shout the guards, as they push at us.

After being in chains for so long, standing, let alone walking, is almost impossible. A girl next to me, Emma, grabs me. Together we pull ourselves up onto our feet.

"This is it," she whispers.

Our eyes lock onto each other, wondering what's next.

Orders yell out for us to move up the stairs. As I step out onto the deck, the sunlight is blinding. Covering my eyes with my arms, I try to shade them from the burning rays.

"Move!" yells one of the guards as he pushes me towards the edge of the deck.

There's so much screaming and yelling it's hard to understand what to do. My legs are weak and shaking as the guard shoves me towards the railing, then orders me to climb over the side and down the rope ladder into a rowboat below. Fear grips me as I stand looking at the ladder. Will I be able to do this? How will I ever hold on?

Suddenly, I feel something hit my back as the guard shoves me forward, nearly knocking me over the edge.

"Get over the side," he says, giving me a shove.

The guards know we'll have trouble going down the ladders. Horrified, I see some prisoners falling into the water, they don't have the strength either. I hear their screams as they thrash around, trying not to drown.

Taking a deep breath, I grab onto the rope ladder and start climbing over the side. I can't hold my grip and fall, but at least I'm partway down and land in the boat.

After the boats are full, the crew rows us towards the shore. The ship hasn't docked in the crowded harbor, but rather some distance offshore from a sandy beach. I look up and see the grey-stone walls of the prison. A group of guards are standing on the beach watching and waiting for us to come ashore.

The two guards in the rowboat orders everyone to stand. Looking around, I'm confused, but do what I'm told. Then without warning one of the guards begins pushing us overboard into the water. I stand screaming as he gives me a shove, and I fall on top of another prisoner, dragging both of us under water.

Nearly drowning, I thrash around gasping for air. I'm so frightened because I can't touch the bottom, and even worse, I barely know how to swim. Choking on the awful saltwater, I struggle to breathe. I don't know how, but maybe the waves push me towards the shore, because soon I find myself touching the sandy bottom. It's then I realize. The guards are using the ocean to bathe us.

The salt water burns my flesh where the shackles have torn into my skin, but still, the cool water is refreshing to the rest of my hurt body. How can something that tastes so bad, feel so soothing? I relish the few minutes I'm given to cleanse. Taking a deep breath, I smell the pure fresh air, filling my lungs to rid myself of the foul stench that I've had to breathe for months.

Defiant, I stand and glare at the prison. *So this is Australia. It doesn't look so bad to me. They say it's dry, barren, and hot, known to be pure hell. On the ship I heard that no one with a life sentence will ever leave this place, they just die here and are buried somewhere out in the desert. Well, they'll see. I may be young, but I'm smart. I'll find a way to escape someday.*

On the beach, the guards herd us closer together, pushing us towards the wagons that are waiting to take us up to the prison. They lock all the men back in irons on their wrists and legs. Ascending the bumpy road to the prison, I feel sad. Looking at the others, they have the same look on their faces as I do. No one talks. We just sit with our spirits broken and ride up the hill.

~~~~~~~~

One at a time the guards pull us from the wagons then shove us into groups. Men on one side, and women on another. A guard grabs my arm and pushes me into the corner with other girls more my age. It's then that I see Emma again. I don't understand why they want to keep us younger girls separate from the older women. Sitting by the prison walls, I see some of the girls crying, while others stare with fright wondering what their fate might be. I don't want to be here either, but I am.

By now I've learnt to mistrust and dislike most men, but that too will be taken to a new level. They've never done anything but treat me badly. I glare at the guards with the same hatred I had at the jail in London. I'm 12 years old now, but time has not helped me see past my rage of pain. It has only increased.

Soon, they force our little group through a doorway that leads to a small dirt yard, away from the rest of the prisoners. I'm thinking maybe they're moving us here to stay until they can figure out what to do with us, but I will soon learn that's not their reason. For now, here we sit waiting in the suffocating Australian heat.

It's dusk, and the hot sun is finally going down. I'm talking to Emma when all of a sudden she grabs my arm and squeezes it tight. I see fear on her face, so I turn to look at what's frightening her. It's a group of guards that are rushing into the yard like a pack of wolves and grabbing some of the girls.

Two guards grab hold of me, throwing me to the ground. One of them pulls up my skirt and rapes me. I hear Emma screaming as guards grab her, raping her too. One after another they come at us, raping us while the others hold us down watching, waiting their turn. I scream and fight, clawing at their faces, and I bite whatever I can sink my teeth into, trying to get away, only to be hit and wrestled back to the ground.

I see their ugly faces. Like a knife carving each one into my memory, I will remember and hate.

As young as we are, they don't care. All they care about is having what they want. We aren't people, we're just nothing but the prize, young flesh they so violently take.

Then it's over, and the guards leave. I grab Emma, moving us into the dark shadows. It's only now that I cry with my friend.

Never did I know men could do such brutal things to a female. I was treated badly at the jail in England, but never this.

The night is long as Emma and I stay close to each other, fearing it will happen again, but it doesn't. Not tonight anyway.

4

The sun begins to rise as we're awakened by guards yelling and ringing a bell. Quickly they herd us through a doorway into a bigger yard where the rest of the prisoners from the ship were kept.

What's it all about?

Emma and I look for a place to sit, far away from everyone.

I notice prisoners starting to line up, and point it out to Emma.

"It must be time to eat. Come on, Adeleen!" she says as she struggles to get up. Yesterday's rapes have made it difficult for us, but painfully and together we make our way in line with everyone else.

No one tells us prisoners what to do, so chaos and confusion are everywhere as the line moves slowly.

With all the shouting, pushing, and shoving, we hold onto each other, trying not to be pushed out. At last Emma and I find ourselves at the front of the line. I'm so hungry. This is the first time we've been given anything to eat since we arrived.

I'm handed a tin plate and stand as slop is scooped into it.

"Now eat up, 'cause 'this is all you scum are gonna get."

One meal a day? Maybe he means for this meal.

"Move on!" someone yells.

Taking a few steps, I stop and glare at the nasty stuff. It looks like what they'd feed to hogs, disgusting maggot-infested gruel.

Someone behind shoves me, causing me to drop my piece of stale bread. Quickly I grab it and hold it close to my body, then look for a place to sit close to Emma. There must be a hopeless look on my face as I stare at what I must eat to stay alive.

Emma sees the disgust on my face, and says, "I don't care, I'm hungry," and picks the maggots from her food and devours the slop with her hands.

I'm hungry too, so, like Emma, flicking the maggots away, I eat.

There's so much wickedness in this prison. It's still daylight, but I sense the darkness of evil engulfing me. Feeling lost, I know I must survive and find a way to escape.

Sadly, like the food, it's only once a day the guards come to fill the large water barrels. If I don't make an effort to get some to drink, then there might not be any left by the end of the day.

Little by little, I understand what I have to do. I see prisoners sick and some dying because they don't have the will to fight for what they need, so they become helpless, and nobody cares.

It's around dusk when the guards start looking over the girls that stay huddled together, to find their choice of victims for the night. I understand now why women are brought to this prison. Talk has it there's probably two-hundred plus guards here at the prison. The men who raped us are only a handful of the guards who will take their turns with us.

My life is already a living hell.

5

I continue to stay in the shadows away from everyone, where it's harder for the guards to see me. I just want to be left alone, although Emma is never far away.

Tonight, two guards stare in my direction pointing and talking. Hopefully, they'll think I'm too much trouble. They want easy targets, not a wild one like me. They probably think I'm mad in the mind, from the way I glare, claw, and bite at them. They could be right; I sometimes wonder myself what I'm becoming. I don't know much about life, but I'm being taught at the worst and hardest school on earth…the prison.

What's going to happen to me? Will I ever go home again? Probably not. But for now I go home in my thoughts and memories. At least there I'm safe.

All prisoners were given a blanket when we first arrived. The nights can get cold, while the days are scorching hot. I have to stay alert. If I lose my blanket, or it gets stolen, I'll have to do without, or take one from someone else. After a few nights I see how important it is to keep it with me all the time. The blankets that are left on the ground get taken. Even while some sleep, their blankets are stolen. Some tie their blanket around their waist, so I do the same, although that doesn't help with the searing heat. I'm glad I have Emma. We can look out for each other.

Three days now, and we're still being held in the yard. There's no place to protect any of us from the hellish sun that scorches our bodies. Even the place where we have to relieve ourselves is degrading, right out in the open for all to watch.

Hordes of annoying flies hover around me, and I'm constantly brushing them away from my face. In the early evening there are the blood-sucking insects. At night, it's the bats diving towards my head scaring me. Everything here wants to either annoy me or eat me.

Another night falling asleep on the ground, hungry and thirsty because I didn't get enough during the day. I hear they might be moving us to a cell tomorrow, but I don't get my hopes up much. I've heard it before, so it's probably a rumor.

❦❦❦❦❦❦

This morning there's a loud commotion outside of the yard. I run with the others to find out what's happening. Standing by the fence, I see strange, small dark-skinned people coming in from the desert. They look so...I don't know what...scary? Who are they?

Walking barefoot, they carry long sharp sticks. They're barely clothed, and their skin looks to be covered in ash, and smeared with white paint. I notice their matted hair, definitely worse than mine. I can't imagine walking with no shoes. Where do these people come from? Who are they?

One of the girls standing by the fence next to me says, "Never seen the likes of them before, have you?"

Looking at her, I shake my head no.

"They come to the prison every once in a while. The guards use them to find escapees or get information about what's going on in the desert. The guards aren't very nice to them either. They treat them like dogs."

"How do you know?" I ask.

"I've seen it," she replies. "I've been here before; this is not my first time at this prison. The guards push them around, like they're worthless, unless they have some valuable information for them. Guards don't care about no one but themselves, you've seen that. They're called the Bush people, because they live out there," pointing to the desert.

15

I turn to look, but can't imagine living beyond the prison walls.

"They're the ones who make that strange sound at night. Kind of eerie," she says.

I nod my head. "Aye, I heard it coming from out there in the dark, but I didn't know what it was."

"They're the people who lived here before the English came. It's too bad they didn't kill the bastard English when they arrived."

Smiling, I think I might have found a new friend. "I'm Adeleen."

"I'm Orla. Where're you from?"

"London. How about you?"

She shrugs, "Oh, I don't remember, maybe from somewhere up north in Scotland. I've been here so long I can't remember much. Me parents were immigrants and somehow came to Australia when I was just a wee one. They're both dead now, but I grew up in the village not too far from here. People took pity on me, and passed me around from family to family. But I was always getting into trouble. Soon nobody wanted me, especially when I was a teen, and their men were always after me, if you know what I mean. I'd get arrested and have to come back to the prison for a time. I don't like Australia. I wish I could go back to Scotland."

I look at her and understand, anywhere but here.

I like my new friend. I can't wait to hear her story, I'm sure she has more to tell.

***

It's day four and the guards are still holding us in the yard. Sitting by Emma in the hot sun, I start to feel sick. My gut aches deep inside. I struggle to make my way over to a corner of the yard, away from everyone, where I want to lie down.

Looking over at the barrel across the yard, I slowly get myself up, and stagger towards it, thinking water might help. If only I can get a drink, I might feel better.

Empty! Those bastards haven't filled the barrel yet. Dropping to my knees beside it, I curl up in a ball.

Looking around I see others just as sick. It must be the rotten pig slop we had to eat that's making us sick.

I close my eyes and try to fall asleep. I hear others talking, but I wouldn't care. Holding my stomach, I lean over and vomit. Over and over again my stomach retches to rid itself of what's making me sick.

Groaning, I slump down in the dirt.

"Move away from the barrel!" barks a guard as he kicks me.

Stumbling to get to my feet, I fall backwards onto the ground.

Pushing me aside and nearly trampling me, the crowd of prisoners rush with their cups to get their water as the guard fills the barrel.

I hear one of the prisoners making a sound. I look up and she's grunting at me, gesturing for me to give her my cup.

I hold my cup close and shake my head no, motioning for her to go away. I don't want to give it to her.

But, she persists and stands tugging at it, trying to pull it from my grip. She's not saying anything, just making a mumbling noise. Too sick to care, I finally let her take it.

Wicked girl stealing my cup. I don't wait to see where she goes, so I lie back down and close my eyes.

A few minutes later someone nudges me. I open my eyes to feel a cup of water touching my lips. I try to gobble it as fast as I can, but she withdraws the cup away, shaking her head as to tell me to sip slower. Then, putting the cup to my lips again, I drink.

Who is she? Is she an Angel? And why isn't she talking? Too sick to find out, I put my head back down.

I recognize Emma's voice whispering to someone. "Is she going to die?"

Not hearing the answer, I roll on my side moaning from my stomach pain.

I don't know how long I lie there, but I feel the guards nudge, or kick at me to see if I'm still breathing. I don't really care, they can leave me to die.

The next day I start feeling better, but still weak and shaky.

"Welcome back to my world," says Emma.

"Thanks. You didn't get sick?"

"No. Remember when we were in line and they dished up the slop into your plate, and then changed pots because it was empty. I ate out of the new pot. Others who ate from the first pot got sick too."

Lucky me.

"Who was that girl with you?" I ask.

Emma shakes her head, and shrugging her shoulders, "I don't know. She doesn't talk very good."

Looking at all the prisoners I try to spot her, but she's nowhere to be found. Emma and I never have seen her again. That's why I think she must have been an Angel.

∾∾∾∾∾

It's hard for me to want to make friends. It frightens me. Maybe because I know their hurt is just as big as mine, and I have a tough time bearing my own. There's an empty hole in my heart, so I'm careful when I let anyone in. I don't want to make friends only to watch them die.

The chance of holding on to life in this hell is probably very slim. Little nourishment, diseases, abuse, and hard labor will be a test of my strength.

Still, I do make a friend. Emma is by me every minute of the day and follows me everywhere. She's two years older than I am, but she's so young in heart. Like me, she doesn't talk much, and I like that. I have nothing to say, and don't really care what others think about anything. But, I can see Emma really needs someone though. Each night she'll sit a little closer to me and soon she has crawled up against me with her back against mine for warmth and comfort. I admit, it does feel better having her close. I guess I do need someone to help me endure this hell.

I'm not responsible for her, I make that plain. I may sound ungrateful after she watched over me when I was sick, but I tell her anyway. She just stares at me and nods.

But I know different, I'll look out for her anyway. I guess I just want to sound tough. I know she needs someone and she's chosen me.

In this prison, I live beyond my sadness. Fighting to stay alive, Emma and I become friends. No strings, just survival.

6

Lying down on the ground for the night, I pull my blanket up to cover my shoulders. I freeze with fear when I see it. It has two pincers and a tail that curls over its back.

Screaming, I throw my blanket aside. Other prisoners run to see what's happening.

"Oh, that'll kill you," says one of the girls, while everyone laughs.

"What the bloody hell is it?" I ask as it scoots away.

"It's a scorpion," someone says.

"Have you seen the giant spiders with the long hair? They'll kill you too," another girl says.

I look at Emma. She's sitting wide-eyed, staring at the thing as it crawls away. Quickly she throws off her blanket. Too frightened to check her own, she kicks it away.

"This place is so evil, Adeleen," cries Emma as tears run down her cheeks. "What are we going to do?"

"Nothing," I snap, while I search through her blanket. "We just have to be more careful," I say, trying to reassure her.

"I don't think I can. I'm scared," cries Emma. "Adeleen, it's going to get on me when I fall asleep!"

Firmly, I take Emma's arms and shake her. "No, it won't, because it knows I'll kill it if it does. Now lie down. I promise, it's gone," I tell her as my eyes scan the dirt for more.

Finally, Emma settles down next to me, but still crying. I'm scared too, but I don't want her to know. Lying close to her, I shut my eyes and try to think of home.

Prisoners gather in groups for safety. If a bunch gets too large though, it can get out of control. Staying by myself is dangerous too. They might think I'm weak, and probably target me and push me around. So, I choose my friends wisely.

Fights occur because someone feels they want to be in charge. There's constant yelling. Nobody talks, they just scream to be heard. The hierarchy among the prisoners is always changing, and I've seen someone killed because of an argument. It helps me to remember, most aren't here because we're nice.

My days have become long and hard. Today the guards plan to assign work to each prisoner. We are told these are the duties we will keep unless they decide otherwise.

After the morning gruel a bell rings, then all the male prisoners are made to form a line. The guards inspect the chains around their ankles before they herd them together into work groups. The men will be kept in chains until they've earned the right to have them removed. Most of the men are going to work at the lime quarry, a dangerous and backbreaking job. I watch as guards shove them forward out through the gate.

Then, orders yell out for us females to form a line. A few minutes later they separate us into groups for jobs throughout the prison.

One group of women are told they have to stay and clean for the guards, while others will have to go scrub floors somewhere.

There's one group that will be going some distance away from the prison to a potato field to dig for roots. This is the job I want to be in. None of the girls want this one because it's hard and heavy work. But I do, I know it will keep me strong.

"I want to try and work someplace inside, out of the searing sun," says Emma. "See you when our day ends, Adeleen."

Nodding to her, I linger as everyone goes to line up.

Emma's quick to get in a line, one she thinks will give her the job she wants, so I watch her push and shove to stay in it.

I walk slowly, so I will be at the back of my line. I know the last group will be the one to go dig. I want to go outside the giant stone walls, if the work doesn't kill me. I plan to hide a root in my clothes for Emma and me to gnaw on tonight, that is, if the guards don't find it. It'll probably taste nasty, but it'll be something extra to eat.

Since arriving I've been passed from one guard to another. I try my hardest to stay out of their sight, but I can't always. I want so desperately to figure out how to stay out of their reach. I look around at the other girls, at all the broken lives, and feel sick. It's been a week of horror.

The days of endless routines start early. I hate being pushed around and told what to do all the time. I struggle a lot with my emotions having to live the way I do. So many times I'm angry and in a bad mood for no reason. I feel myself changing, and I wonder why my friend Emma still likes me, because I don't anymore.

Walking has become difficult for me. I've outgrown my shoes, but I won't let that stop me from going out to dig. I slip my feet into the toes and smash the heels down to make them fit. It's uncomfortable, but I have no choice, I will have to endure the discomfort. When I ask for another pair of shoes, the guards laugh. One of them says he would get me a pair, but that was days ago, so I don't really believe him. Too afraid to ask again, I do what I can to make what I have work.

Who knows if I will ever get another pair?

7

The root patch is down a narrow path across the red dirt, over rocks and past the thorn bushes. It's quite a walk out towards the Australian desert.

On the other side of the prison, there are apple trees, but of course they never take us there. I think they want to make us suffer.

Today there are twelve of us walking together with one guard. This work group is one of the few times where they have men and women prisoners work together.

A rustling in the bushes startles me. Suddenly, strange large animals cross in front of us. They're like giant rabbits with long tails. They hop across the road, and then quickly back into the brush. What are these creatures?

Not wanting us to stop, the fat guard comes up behind me and another girl and gives us both a shove. "Hurry up, you sweet things, or I'll feed you to 'em," he laughs.

The guard grimaces as he tries to ignore today's heat. It's obvious it's getting to him from the looks of the sweat running down his red face.

What'd he do to get this awful job? The poor sap. I can't help but hope the heat will kill him. I glare back at his ugly face, then keep walking.

"Don't you hate this place?" a voice yells from ahead.

I look up and see it's one of the male prisoners.

"This country's straight from hell!" he screams loudly.

What is he doing?

Hearing the loud voice, the guard pushes his way through the group to see what's going on.

"Hell! That's where we are, HELL!" The prisoner then starts heading into the desert. "HELL! HELL!" he screams again.

Running up behind him, the guard yells for him to stop. Not heeding the warning, he continues to go crazy. Using the back of his rifle, the guard gives him a hard blow to his back, knocking him to the ground. It does little to stop him from screaming. Reaching around grabbing his back where the guard struck him, he struggles to get to his knees, still screaming "HELL!"

Then with a rifle blow to back of his head, I hear his skull crack and he falls to the dirt.

"Pick him up!" yells the guard. "We're going back. Now hurry it up and do it!"

Two men lift him up, as the guard pushes at us to turn us back towards the prison. The man lies limp in their grip. *Is he dead?* I hurry with the group, trying to stay out of the angry guard's way.

The infernal heat feels like the sun is burning up all the air, making it difficult to breathe. A hot wind suddenly starts to blow stirring up dirt up from the ground. I pull part of my skirt up to cover my mouth to keep from choking. The dust gets so thick I can hardly see where to go.

"Get moving, unless you wish'in' to die out here!" shouts the guard.

Stumbling, I walk right out of one of my shoes. When I stop to reach back and get it, the guard pushes me onward.

"My shoe!" I scream.

"Forget it!" he yells, shoving me forward.

Crying, I stumble back towards the group. Through the dust I see one of the girls reaching out to give me her hand. I grab on while keeping my head down, trying to protect my face. Who is this girl?

Even though we aren't supposed to talk to one another, I whisper, "Thanks."

The trek back seems even longer. My foot starts to bleed from stepping on sharp rocks and desert briers.

Finally, we're back at the yard, and I find a place where I can sit to pick the thorns from my foot. Blood mixed with the red dirt makes for a real mess. My foot throbs with pain as I lift it up on my lap. "God, it hurts." Picking at it, I try to pull out what's imbedded. Dropping my head, nearly ready to give up, I take a deep breath and continue. As I'm sitting there, a shadow comes over me, blocking the sunlight that has returned after the dust storm. Looking up, I see the same girl who helped me walk back.

Squatting down beside me, she says, "I'm Liz."

"I'm Adeleen. Thanks for helping me. It sure was a bloody hell of a walk back for me."

Liz looks at my foot and winces at the sight. "Ew, it looks like it hurts. I can help pull those thorns out if you want. What are you going to do with no shoe?" she asks as she pulls another thorn.

Thinking about it for a minute, I say, "All I can do is tie something around it. Maybe tomorrow on my way back out I can find my shoe."

"We have nothing. What are you going to use?" Liz asks.

Reaching for the bottom of my skirt, I rip a strip off, and then wrap the bit of cloth around my foot. I shrug, "It's a rag anyway, and a few more tears won't matter. There! See, that should work."

Liz smiles with approval. "When we came back, I went over and asked how the crazy man was. They told me he died."

"I thought that might be, I heard his skull crack when the guard slammed his rifle to his head." *A flashing memory of me hitting my father.* Shaking it away, I go back to talking with Liz.

"I've been watching you," says Liz. "You don't give up. You fight and stand up for yourself. That's good. The guards push me around a lot, but I don't have the nerve to do anything. I'm too afraid,"

"I understand," I tell her.

"I hear they're moving us to our cells tomorrow. Wonder what that will be like," she says.

"Probably just another part of this castle," I say sarcastically.

We both laugh, although we aren't happy about anything.

Emma makes her way over to where I'm sitting. "What's happening?"

"Oh, I lost one of my shoes. I can't wait until those bastards find me another pair to wear."

"You know where our shoes and clothes come from, don't you?" says Liz.

"No," I answer.

"They take them off dead people. I've seen 'em. They strip them right where they die."

I look at her then turn away. *This is hell*, I whisper to myself.

❧❧❧❧❧

I hang my head in anguish. I feel so lost and ashamed from what's happening to me. I don't want to be here and be forced to be a woman. I just want to go home where I can feel safe and be a little girl again.

Sitting alone, I think back to my home in England. I imagine seeing Benjamin with the cows, and Mum hanging the fresh-washed clothes on a line. I twirl as my dress lifts in the breeze. My life was simple and happy. How I long to be there again.

My thoughts are the only things that are mine alone. They're something this prison will never take from me. When I dare close my eyes, I am with my memories anytime I want. Living within my thoughts is my only comfort in this vile place.

My nights are frightening. Most of the time, I lie awake too afraid to fall asleep. All through the night, I hear noises from the desert that keep me awake. Clutching tight to my blanket, I listen to the yelping and howling from the wild dogs. It's terrifying. I can tell when they make a kill, and I cringe every time I hear it. Sometimes it's the agonizing cries from their prey, along with the yelps and howls from the pack. It's an ungodly, unnerving sound that makes me shiver because I know something is being ripped apart. Maybe it's a desert hopper, or maybe one of the bush people. It might even be a prisoner who has decided to try an escape. It's a really good reason for me to re-think if I ever want to try an escape through the desert.

8

The guards tell us today is the day we'll be taken to our cells. We've been living in the yard for weeks, so I'm eager to find out what they're like. I don't know why, but I think I'll feel safer knowing I'll be behind those iron bars. Maybe it's because of those wild dogs.

Orders yell for all us women to line up along the fence. Emma and I make our way over and stand aside as the men, still bound with heavy chains on their wrist and ankles, are taken first through the gate into the main prison.

"Come on ladies. It's your turn," says a guard with a big smirk on his face.

"What is he smiling about?" I ask Emma. She shakes her head as we move on with the others.

The guards push our line through the gate onto a path that leads towards a building. A different direction than the men were taken. I hear yelling coming from ahead.

"Get in there!" orders a guard, forcing us through an open door. Suffocating smells and foul words greet us as we are paraded into the men's cell block.

"This is where they keep the crazies," someone yells.

Horrified, I look ahead and see a gantlet of arms stretching out from behind iron bars ready to reach out and grab us. Huddling close to the girl in front of me I try to follow along, while Emma hangs on behind me. All we can do is shuffle our feet at a slow pace. Hands reach out as fingers brush against our skirts and arms. A woman shoves the line, causing one girl to stumble and fall towards the horrifying men who are quick to grab onto her. No one dares to reach out to help her. I hear loud piercing screams and see others stumbling before me, but quickly they're able to right themselves.

Terrified, the girl struggles to get free from the hands that latch onto her. They yank at her hair, bloodying her head from banging it against the cell bars. Hands grab her legs and arms, ripping at her clothes in an attempt to pull her in through the narrow openings.

The guards laugh and seem to enjoy taunting the male prisoners with us females. Finally they get around to pulling the poor bloody girl from the terrorizing grips, and push her back to the line.

I feel fingers brushing my arms, causing a horrifying sensation to run through me. Emma and I hang onto each other, gripping tight, hoping we don't fall or get separated. I scream in horror. I want to close my eyes and ears and hide like a little girl to make this all go away.

⁂

Our cell is in a large room with a heavy iron door that gives a loud, unnerving sound as it slams shut. I see bunks bolted to the walls throughout the room. The guard points to a smelly drain-hole in the floor that's out in the open.

"This is where you'll go to shit. If you're lucky, once a day someone will come with a bucket of water and wash the mess down the drain, but you'll still smell your stench," he says, enjoying his introduction.

Not waiting to hear any more from the sickening guard, I rush past the girls, pushing my way through, and run to the far end of the cell away from the stench of the drain. I jump into one of the bunks on the wall and wait for Emma. I see her and wave as she makes her way through the chaos. I was quick enough to get the lower bunk against the wall. We sit and watch Liz and Orla grab their bunk. We wave at them to let them know where we are. They're both older than Emma and me, but I like them, and so my group of friends grows.

It isn't a big cell given the number of prisoners they cram in here. The women are like dogs fighting one another for beds. Two older

28

women loudly voice their objections to the bed Emma and I got, but soon they give up arguing with us and move to another bed, where they make someone move.

We give them our meanest glare — as if two young girls might frighten them. Still nobody's moving us, and they know it. The old sows.

Anyway, we're the youngest ones of the group, and no one else says anything. Maybe they've heard the story that I've killed someone. Even so, we get to keep the bunk we want, and here we stay.

We have no mattresses, just wood planks to lie on, still, it's better than the dirt. Two women grab the bed above us, but we don't know them. I wish Orla and Liz had gotten it.

Our bed is hardly big enough to fit the two of us comfortably, but some have three to a bunk, or else someone has to sleep on the concrete floor, and nobody wants that.

I hear a high-pitched scream coming from the other end of our cell. Girls crawl over one another trying to get away from something. It's a giant spider the size of my hand creeping up through the drain hole and slowly moving across the floor.

Emma and I sit on our bunk pulling our feet up, and watch one brave girl run over to smash the spider, killing it. Blood-curdling screams fill the cell as hundreds of baby spiders scatter in every direction.

It must have been a female spider carrying an egg sac. I watch in horror as some of the tiny spiders come in our direction, so I hop from my bunk and start stomping on them. Emma shrieks but she's too frightened to help.

Some of the girls are able to smash some, but there are too many and soon they disappear in crevices and under the bunks. There's no way we can kill them all, which means — they're in our cell. It'll take days before I'll feel safe from the spiders, but still, I'm always looking for them.

One girl tells me that this country has lots of deadly bugs.

"Best not get bitten by any," she says, "You might not live. Your flesh will just eat away and rot off your bones."

Well, that's comforting to know. Why is this land so cursed?

My first night inside the cell is especially frightening. I lie in my bunk clutching my blanket as I ache with sadness and fear. I think about the spiders, then listen to the haunting screams coming from throughout the prison. Sometimes the screams come from women and other times men.

I roll towards Emma and find comfort having her close. How will I ever stay alive in this damnable place?

9

In the morning, just before the sun comes up, I'm startled awake by the guards yelling as they bang their sticks back and forth across the iron bars. It's such a racket that I wake up with my heart pounding.

Through all the confusion a line soon forms. This time they don't take us past the men's cells where the arms are sticking out. Instead they shuffle us down a long, dark walkway towards another building. Frightened at what might be next, I tell Emma to stay close.

As we walk in through two open wooden doors, I see tables and benches across the room and another line of prisoners waiting to get food. Emma and I make a dash to join them.

"What's it going to be?" asks Emma.

"I don't know, probably that same slop we got in the yard," I answer.

I look around the room and feel depression fill me. Is this where I'm going to have to eat with my hands for the rest of my life? I don't want to live. Maybe I'll be lucky and choke on the mash.

As the line moves forward, we see the food.

"It ain't so bad," says Emma.

"Shut up," I grumble.

She glares at me, and then changes her mind about making a smart remark.

"I don't want to be here," I say, as tears spring from my eyes.

"Me either," she says, "but we are, so you shut up."

Taking my dress sleeve I wipe the snot from my nose and face, I look directly into her eyes. "Emma, where is your bravery coming from? You almost sound like me."

I start to snicker, and then we both laugh. There isn't anything to laugh about, only maybe Emma's newly found bravery. Am I rubbing off on her? I hope so.

When I get back to our cell I continue to look for the spiders. Over time it seems to be clear of them, but we never know for sure.

It's close to sundown and time for the guards to come in and take the girls they want for the night. It isn't until after they've gone that the rest of us can all relax.

"Emma, what are you going to do when you get out of here?"

"I don't know, I just got here. That's a long ways off for me to even think about it."

"You only have a ten-year sentence. I have life. But, I'm not going to stay here. Someday, somehow, I'm getting out."

"Dead maybe," say Emma.

"No, I'm going to find a way, I can promise you that, and it won't be in a wooden box."

"Adeleen, there's no way out of here. You heard everyone."

"Not yet, but I'll find it."

"Hmmm," says Emma.

Our friends, Orla and Liz, come to sit with Emma and me so we can talk and share our stories. I think it's one of the few times we all can laugh.

I'm starting to learn more each day about my new friends. Not all the stories make us laugh though. Many are sad, and I feel their pain, but after we get the hurt behind us, we begin to laugh again. So, I get to know them, and they get to know me too.

Orla is the first to share about her life. She's older than Emma and me, but she fits right in with our lot. She much like Emma. She has no deep feelings of revenge, like I do. I want to get even with anyone who harms me, but she doesn't, she surrenders to whatever happens. She says nothing changes if she strikes back, it can only make things worse. If they hit her, and she hits them back, she knows they'll hit her even harder. So, she doesn't fight.

"I was sent to this prison before, when I was fifteen. They gave me a five-year sentence for stealing. When I got out, I had nowhere to go, so I stole again to survive, but got caught. Here I am, back in prison again. Now, I'm serving another five years," Orla tells us.

I don't understand why Orla didn't learn her lesson. Who would want to come back to this horrible place? To get out and be sent back baffles me. She tells us she is good at what she does, but that's stupid, because she's in here. God, how I wish I could have a chance to get out. I know I'd never do anything that would bring me back again.

Liz on the other hand, doesn't want to talk about why she's here. Maybe it's something bad and in time she'll share.

Then Emma shares her story. I think she doesn't deserve to be here. She was sent here because of false accusations. Just looking at Emma, I don't understand why someone wanted to get rid of her. She is pretty, tiny, and gentle.

"A wealthy couple hired me after my parents died," she tells us. "They worked me as a servant at their huge estate. It was a beautiful manor house in the countryside of Yorkshire. I loved working there, until the master started misbehaving. The mistress of the house didn't like the attention I was getting from him. Then one afternoon she caught him standing close behind me caressing my curls and smelling my hair as I was feather dusting. It was quite a scene. Later I heard them fighting, and she was threatening to get rid of me. I knew it was going to be just a matter of time. I don't know why she didn't just dismiss me. But instead, she accused me of stealing. Any time there were repeat offenses, you're labeled as defective and sent to prison. The master didn't even try to come to my defense."

"Dirty bastard!" says Liz.

We all nod.

Then there's Yuliya — someone told me she's from a country they call Russia, wherever that is. Nobody knows what she's in prison for, but I don't care. I like her very much. I think she's my age, or maybe older, but she's sassy just like me. She doesn't take guff off of anybody. She works mostly in the kitchen and sometimes smuggles bread back for Emma and me. She makes me laugh. She doesn't speak or understand English very well. She just smiles and nods her head a lot. She is easy to like.

"What about you, Adeleen?" my friends ask. "Tell us your story."

What will they think of me when I share with them? I take a deep breath, and then tell them how I killed my father when I was nine years old by hitting him in the head with a hammer." I hear the girls gasp, but continue. "I only hit him once, and that was because I was afraid of him."

I tell them the whole story and wait for more reactions. "And that's all it took. Slam went the gavel, then the iron door closing behind me. I was so stupid."

They all stare at me for a minute, trying to believe what I was telling them.

Orla speaks up. "You did right, Adeleen. I would've hit him too."

And Liz agrees, nodding her head.

Hearing my friends' say that makes me feel better, a kind of acceptance. Everyone except Emma, that is. She looks at me with disbelief and says nothing.

Please don't let me lose Emma.

❦❦❦❦❦❦

It's been five days since the dust storm, and my shoe is nowhere to be found. It's probably buried under tons of dirt.

Still limping, it's difficult for me to walk the distance to the dig. I know the guards will eventually stop me, and they do. Today, I wouldn't be going.

"You…move to the other line!" yells one of the guards.

I don't want to stop, so I pretend not to hear him. Without looking at him I keep walking.

"Stop!" he yells as he pushes others out of his way to get over to me. "You heard me!" He grabs me and shoves me towards another group of women. "Now move!"

One of the redcoat lieutenants from the military attachment reaches out. "No, she's not. She's coming with me," he says, taking my arm.

Oh no. Fearing the worst, I pull back.

Dragging me with him, he says, "I'm not going to hurt you," as he tightens his grip on my arm.

Stopping at the door, he reaches and opens it, pulling me inside. I continue to try to pull away. I've never made it easy for any of them to rape me, and I'm not going to make it easy for him either. Leaning around I sink my teeth into his hand.

"Quit it, you hellion!" he yells.

Having been passed from man to man makes me mistrust them all. So I kick him, aiming at his man parts.

"Stop it!" he yells, slapping me.

The guards in the room laugh at the difficulty I give him. Red coat or not, I continue to try an bite him.

Giving me a heave, he throws me against the wall.

Yelling at one of the guards, "Get her some shoes, and make sure they fit!"

My eyes widen as the raging fight within me calms. Afraid to speak, I stand quiet with caution.

"She's quite a wildcat, ain't she?" one says.

"That she is, she's pretty wild," the lieutenant says, "but I think she'll settle down now."

Too afraid to get close to me, one of the guards throws three pairs of shoes at me. "See if any of these fit."

Slowly, still glaring at them, I lower myself onto the floor. The guards laugh as they watch me try on the shoes.

I'm so glad you swine are enjoying yourselves.

Then sadly, I remember what Liz told me. I wonder who died. I find a pair of boots, thinking they will be better out in the desert.

Not wanting to stay any longer, I get up and bolt out the door.

"Let her go," I hear the lieutenant behind me say. "Let them put up with her."

Outside, my work group has already gone.

"You're going here," says one of the guards as he points to the girls who go to wash floors.

I look and see Emma getting her pail and brush. Quickly, I cut into line right behind her.

"Can't go dig?" whispers Emma.

"Nope, but I got some new boots," I say as we both look down at the badly worn boots. Emma looks at me and we both smile.

"Fancy," she whispers.

❦❦❦❦❦❦

There are many days I wake up angry. My moods are difficult for me to control. I don't understand why, but I just want to fight. My sharp tongue cuts into anyone who gets in my way. Most avoid me when I'm this way, especially Emma. She's smart enough to stay clear. Best not bother me.

I don't like it when the hate wells up within me like this, but it seems to be there just below the surface. Sometimes, it doesn't take much to set me off.

There's one prisoner who gets under my skin. Her name is Margaret — a crusty older woman who's loud and ugly. When she laughs, she cackles like an annoying chicken. Every time I see her, I try to avoid her. She's bossy and pushy, and thinks she's in charge, telling everyone what to do and how to do it, getting in your face and belittling you.

No one has the nerve to stand up to her, so they laugh, but all the while, they want her to go away. The guards never do anything to stop her. In fact, I think they enjoy seeing everyone cower to her. She's smelly and missing most of her front teeth, which were probably knocked out in a fight. The teeth that are left are rotting in her mouth and her breath…you don't want to get too close. The smell will make you gag.

Everyone at the prison has different jobs, so when it's time for the guards to move us in lines, Margaret starts to bark out orders telling everyone to get in line and straighten up. No one knows who put her in charge, or if anyone has. She just has the need to run everything. Today, I'm in no the mood for her. As I walk to go out the gate, she promptly jumps in my face.

She's made the mistake I've been waiting for. "Get out of my way, you old hag," I say, egging her on.

"Where do you think you're going?" she demands.

"Move your foul self before I rip your horse face off!" I yell.

Shoving my way past her, I knock her aside. Margaret grabs my hair to stop me. Turning around, I reach up to scratch her dried-up, ugly face.

"Let go of me, you pig!" I scream as I bite her arm.

Next thing I know, we're rolling around on the ground clawing at each other. I hear all the girls crowding around yelling as we fight. I grab a handful of dirt and smash it into her face, causing her to spit.

"Eat that, you fat sow!" I shriek.

Grabbing her by the hair, I pull her sideways back into the dirt. I jump on her back and grab her around the throat, squeezing, hoping to make her stop breathing. It takes everything I have not to kill her, even though I want to.

Pushing her face into the ground, I feel her grab my leg and toss me back to the ground. Swinging her fist, she clobbers me on my right cheek. I taste blood, but I don't care. When I'm done with her, she won't have a face. With my fist, I strike a hard blow to her chin. All of a sudden she falls limp.

"Get up, you ugly dog! Just try barking at me again!" I scream as I kick dirt on her. Margaret lies quiet on the ground. I don't know if she's is hurt or just faking it to stop the fight, but I don't care. Either way, I got her out of my face.

Wiping the blood from my face, I leave her there in the dirt and walk away.

Fights are an everyday occurrence, although I'm often left alone. I look around at everyone watching — they know that I'm not the innocent girl I was when I first arrived. I'm older now, and have a reputation. Most know that if they tangle with me, they will probably get hurt. They understand that I know how to fight and Margret knew it too, but she just had to try, hoping to find me weak, but she was wrong. Now maybe she'll shut that loud hole. I know that won't happen, but I'm sure someday someone will shut it, and shut it for good.

10

We've been told by the older women that it could happen, and it has. One of the girls who was raped the first day we got here is going to have a baby. We were all told by one of the older women to watch for our blood to come each month. If it does, then we should be safe, but if not, then there might be a baby. She also taught us to stuff whatever we can and hold between our legs to keep the blood from dripping on the floor. If the guards were to see it, they'd beat us.

Emma and I find out it's Yuliya, our Russian friend, who is the one going to have a baby. Emma and I really like her, even though she's gruff. Most of the other girls don't like her, but we don't care, we do. I know Yuliya likes us. She's always nodding her head and smiling at us, which must mean something. At night, when we're in our bunk, Emma and I can see her and wonder how much longer before we'll see a baby. When she notices us looking in her direction, she just smiles and waves. Over time Yuliya's belly grows and grows. How much bigger is it going to get?

My work crew has finished early today so I get to go back to my cell. I hear someone crying. I look, and it's Yuliya. She's bent over holding her stomach and reaching out wanting me to help her. Grabbing onto me, she points at her bunk. I help to support her as we make our way over to it.

One of the older women shoves me aside. "Get outta my way. I've got er', missy."

Giving her a hard look, I let go.

It must be time! Excited, I rush off to find Emma. I push my way through the others who are coming back in from work and search for her.

"Hey, watch it!" one yells as I bump into her.

Grabbing Emma, "The baby, I think it's coming out!" I say with excitement.

Eager to see what it's all about, we hurry over to our bunk where we get a clear view of what is about to happen. I have never seen anyone give birth before, not even an animal, so I'm curious, and excited. There is so much of life I don't understand, but I'm soon to get an education I'll never forget.

Some of the older women are arguing. Yuliya doesn't understand what they're saying. She looks confused. Why are they fighting over her? I hear them telling Yuliya she should go with the guards now that it's her time. But others say don't because they've heard she won't come back with her baby.

Poor Yuliya looks so frightened. They need to stop arguing and shut up.

Emma and I watch as Yuliya goes through the long labor and horrific pains of childbirth. I see how afraid she is by the way she holds onto the older women. She's young like me, and I'm sure she doesn't understand either. Emma and I huddle together in our bunk listening to Yuliya scream. Why does it hurt so much? Emma and I don't even talk. I guess the shock of it all makes us quiet.

She suffers for hours and gets even louder as her labor continues. I grow tired from hearing her, so I try to drown them out like when I was a little girl, by putting my fingers in my ears and humming a song. But, it does little to stop me from hearing her agonizing screams because we're locked in our cell, and there's nowhere to go to find quiet.

All of a sudden Yuliya's screams stop and I hear the baby cry. Emma and I look at each other and sit up on our bunks trying to see her baby. With everyone crowding around, it's impossible. So, Emma and I take each other's hand and get off our bunk, trying to move closer. Too scared to let go, we cling to each other, pushing our way over, then finally we get close enough to see her tiny little baby. It's making a soft little cry as it lies cradled in her arms.

We watch as the women continue to help Yuliya. There's something coming out from between her legs that's still attached to her baby. Turning away I can't look any more and gag at the sight of all the blood. Then I take a deep breath and look back.

One of the women says she needs something to cut the cord. Another finds a strip of cloth and uses it to tie tightly around it. Why are they doing that? Another woman goes over to the guard and asks if she can use something to cut the cord, but comes back with nothing.

Yuliya struggles again. Is it another baby? No, it's the afterbirth, someone says. What a disgusting glob of bloody flesh. After it comes out, one of the women pulls the cord until it severs from the glob, then takes it over to the stench hole and drops it in.

The tiny baby's cries are barely heard over all the noise from everyone in the cell. We only get a glimpse of the baby before Yuliya gets upset and starts screaming at everyone.

"No!" she pleads. Clutching her baby to her breast, she waves for everyone to get away.

Emma and I run back to our bunk. I should understand more, but I don't. It's so scary and sad. I look at Emma and together we both cry. Tired and frightened from it all, I lie down and worry. How long before I too will go through this same horror as Yuliya? I don't say anything to Emma, but she might be thinking the same thing.

So what happens to the babies born at the prison? I don't know.

The guards don't care about the mums or their babies. They don't want any of their bastard babies to live anyway. I wonder, do they ever think it might be theirs? Either way, there are no children at the prison. Why?

That morning we walk quietly past Yuliya and her tiny baby on our way out to work. But by evening when we came back, her baby is gone. I see Yuliya all curled up in a corner on her bunk, sleeping. The talk is, the guards came and took it from her.

How sad. Seeing a woman give birth in prison is horrible, but to take away her baby is even crueler. I realize there will be many more births as I look around and see more women with swollen bellies.

His breath stinks of liquor as I feel it on the back of my neck. Wrapping his arms around my waist he demands, "Come here, you young thing."

"Leave her alone, you've had enough!" yells the senior guard, Hughes, approaching rapidly.

"Aw, I just wanna have some fun," the vile guard says while holding me tight in his grip and pulling me against his repulsive body.

"Get away from her, I tell you." Grabbing me by my wrist, Hughes pulls me free.

There's no mercy shown to any of us girls. These men always fight over us. The only reason we're here at the prison is to take care of their disgusting needs.

Tugging at me, Hughes, the ugly senior guard, roughly pushes me toward his quarters.

"You'll be with me from now on, so stay away from the others," says Hughes harshly.

And so my ownership begins. But I know with the next shipment of females, he'll probably tire of me and choose another. I've seen it happen many times to other girls. How long will I stay with him? Only he knows. In many ways, I'm somewhat lucky. To be chosen by someone is actually safer. The other guards won't be able to pass me around. Not all the girls are so fortunate, or is it good fortune? I'll find out.

I'm 15 now and for the last three years have been used by many men. He's the first guard to take and keep me. The scars on his face tell stories of the fights he's been in. He's a cruel man, and I'm not given luxuries of any kind — like I would expect any. Each night when he's through with me, I'm to sleep, like a dog, with a blanket on the floor in the corner of his room.

I don't know how I'll get through this, but I will. I just need to keep looking for a way to escape.

Hughes tells me if I cause him any trouble, he'll beat me. I'm to clean and scrub for him, get food for him, and, of course, his bed. I think I'd rather be beaten and sent back with the rest of the girls, but he keeps me for himself for about a month before losing interest.

He eventually sees another guard with a girl he likes better and immediately pulls rank and takes her for himself. He isn't liked by any of the guards, and often finds himself having to push his way around just to keep fear in them. It doesn't matter, I'm glad to get back to my cell with my friends…at least for now.

✤✤✤✤✤✤

My days have run into months, and then years, but I never give up trying to find a way to get out of here. I know someday I will leave this place and escape.

I have learned to behave and not fight the guards so much. They begin to trust me, and now give me jobs that allow me more freedom. My life isn't my own anymore, so in my mind I grow deadened and detach myself from what I can. I don't want to feel, so I have become nothing, showing very little emotion.

I only trust Emma to tell my hurt to, but she has her own pain. So I don't always burden her. It's difficult, I don't fully trust anyone else, and nobody cares what anyone is going through anyway.

I'll never know what's kept me from having a child these first few years. The guards have grabbed me time and time again. Maybe I'm too young, but Yuliya was young. Maybe it's my wild side, my fighting hatred of these men that keeps my body from conceiving. I don't know.

Over and over again I see more women with their bellies swollen. I still don't know where some of them go to give birth. No one wants to talk about it, and no one ever comes back with a baby. It's just something that is.

There are times some of the women are driven crazy from their loss. Those rat-bastard men! How I hate them all for doing this.

Eventually, I do become pregnant — it's inevitable. I think of the little life beginning inside me and feel sad. Several months into my pregnancy, the blood begins to flow, signaling a miscarriage. It's at night when my unrelenting pain begins, and by morning it's over.

42

Several of the girls stay by my side throughout the night. They understand. They know my anguish, and remember their own. I see sadness in their faces and understand. The next morning they tell the guard I'm sick, so I'm left alone to sleep, alone to quietly cry.

❧❧❧❧❧

Australia is an extremely harsh country. The summer days are hot and sweltering. The relentless heat bakes our bodies like an oven. The prison is on the western side of this giant land. Every day around the same time in the afternoon, a wind will blow in from the ocean. They call this breeze *The Doctor* because it makes everyone feel better. It isn't cool, but it moves the air, and that is a welcome relief. It's hellish hot here, but the breeze moving over our sweat makes it bearable.

The winters can be harsh too. Whenever the temperature drops, which doesn't happen very often, the same winds can become a monster. It brings the storms in off the ocean, dampening all in its path. At times I've gotten a chill that hurts all the way to my bones. I don't know which I dislike worse, summer or winter. Well, that's no question, I hate everything about being here.

I think back to the black London winters of my childhood, remembering the suffocating plumes of smoke hanging in the air from the coal burners, making breathing difficult. I think everyone walked around with a cough. I know I did. The snow there wasn't white either. It was blackened from all the ash. I don't remember seeing much of the sun in the winter. I think it stayed hidden behind the dirty soot-filled clouds. How I long for home, and I probably always will.

My life changes over time. I can't always go to dig outside the walls where I can be in the desert, but when I do, I like it. Most of the time, I only get to see the desert from high up on the prison walls when I take the guards their water. I understand and have learned to accept that my life won't become anything. Having a life sentence in prison has robbed me of any kind of goals or hopes, for all I have is today. So when I get to go out to dig, I'm as happy as I can make myself. I let my mind take me home, and picture myself digging in my mum's beautiful garden.

I'm not overjoyed, don't get me wrong. The endless days with the same routine I have learned to live with. I do try to make the most of my ugly life, even if I am digging in the red Australian dirt.

Today I get to go out to dig. While digging for potato roots, my tool hits something. My eyes widen as I unearth something made of metal. It's a small dagger. How is it that it came to be buried out here beside a rock? Part of the handle is broken away, and it's rusty from being in the earth, but it's a knife all right. Carefully, I look around to see if anyone else is watching. It's risky, hiding something like this. If I get caught, it'll mean a terrible beating, or maybe worse. But that's something I'm willing to risk.

Looking over at the guard, I see he's walking away in the other direction. Still sitting, I quickly move the knife beneath my dress, then slowly slide it into my boot.

It's just what I need. I can use it when I escape, or better yet, rip into the guts of the guards as they come to rape me. I let my imagination take me as I continue to dig, my mind is full of thoughts of revenge...

...He comes at me like all other times.

"Come here, sweetheart," he says as he takes his time looking me over. Tossing me on my back, he pulls me under him and raises my skirt. I look at him with a slight smile, as he lowers himself onto me. Then with a quick movement of my wrist, I split his belly.

"Ahhhh! Ahhh!" he gasps as he grabs his stomach. With blood gushing, he lifts himself from me as his innards fall from his gut. He looks at me, and then collapses dead.

"Ha, ha," I whisper.

Yes, I need what I've found. I might be too afraid to use it, but for now I'll keep it hidden and continue to endure the assaults. Just knowing that if I really need to use it gives me hope. I'm not going to tell my friends, not even Emma.

Returning from the dig, as usual a guard stops us to search everyone to see if anyone is hiding anything. I know the routine, so why would I hide something where you can find it?

No, you dogface scum, it's in my boot.

Dropping my basket on the table and lifting my arms so I can be searched, I glare at the guard. Then head off to my cell.

❦❦❦❦❦

Entering my cell, I hurry to hide my knife. I don't see Emma. She must be with a guard for the night. Hearing Orla and Liz giggling over in their bunk, I can't help but be curious. There isn't much to laugh about in this place, so what's making them so happy?

"What's going on?"

Orla looks at Liz, and then they reveal to me something they're hiding. It's a small jug of the guards' grog they've stolen. Putting their foreheads together, they snicker, making sure to keep the jug hidden from sight.

"How in the world…?"

I'd never tasted strong drink, or any other spirits for that matter. Eager to be as happy as they are, I ask, "Can I have some?"

Motioning for me to sit, Liz scans the cell to see if anyone is aware of what they have. Sitting beside me, Orla slowly moves the small jug towards me. This is exciting. I too look around to see how many are watching and wait for any to turn away, then, hiding behind Orla I take a big gulp. Suddenly, I struggle to breathe.

Coughing and sputtering from the burn, I gasp, "This is wicked stuff, where did you get it?"

"Oh, you don't need to know," Liz says as she grins.

Hiding behind Orla, I take a second swig. "Blimey, it's strong," I struggle to say without my breath.

"Don't drink it all. Here, give it back," says Orla reaching out for the jug.

"Just once more." I turn my shoulder away to stop her from taking it, downing another swallow, this time not so much. Feeling a burn all the way down to my stomach, I sit back as a warmth travels down my arms. I look at one of the other women in the cell and giggle. Her eyes narrow as she looks straight at me.

"What are you laughing at?" she demands.

Smirking, I say, "Not, you." Then I hear Orla and Liz snickering too.

"I guess she doesn't like what I said," I told my friends.

Uh-oh. That must have been the wrong thing to say. I watch her jaw clench as she walks straight over to me. Getting in my face, she understands the reason for everything.

"Hey! These girls got some rot. I can smell it!" she shouts to the others in the cell.

"Go 'way, you just never mind and go crawl back over to your dog bed," says Orla, giving her a shove.

Oh, no! I wait, knowing what's about to happen.

"Fight!" someone screams.

Grabbing my hair the girl hits me. But, that's fine with me, I want to punch her too. Chaos erupts. Everyone begins to fight. I think we all need to clobber someone, sometimes.

Feeling a hit to the back of my head, I see bright lights and black dots. The next thing I know, the guards are pulling me out of the cell.

Standing against a wall, the three of us wobble, trying to stay upright. I, with my swollen eye and lip, Orla bleeding from her nose, and Liz, well, she has scratches all over her face.

"So, you're the ones who stole my rum," says one of the guards as he inspects his empty jug.

"Well, these girls ought to be fun, don't you think?" says Hecox as he leads Liz away.

"At least they're in a good mood."

We know what's about to happen. They're going to take us and have their way, and afterwards walk us over for a lashing. That is if we're not friendly enough. Feeling the way I do at this moment, I can be very friendly. They should give us drink more often. It might make it more pleasant for them. But, right now I don't care about their punishment. It was worth it to feel good and drunk for a little while.

Once sober, it's back to reality, and back to hell. And, no, we didn't get a lashing.

11

Scrubbing the floors isn't my favorite job. I'd rather be outside the walls, where I can breathe the fresh air. But that isn't always to be.

While walking over to my group who usually goes out to dig, one of the guards shouts at me, but I pretend not to pay attention. He's decided to change my job, something I always feared could happen. Grabbing me by the nape of my neck, he shoves me towards a different line. I remember this line from before, when I lost my shoe and couldn't go dig. It's the one Emma's in.

Looking back at him, I smile as if this is exactly where I want to be. *But it's not.*

The girls who do this work are tattered from the hardships and abuse. Even Emma looks worn. Each of us has a desire to live, though. Funny how that is — we can be put in the worst of conditions, but we find it within ourselves an inner need to stay alive.

On my knees, today's labor is hard. I'm not used to scrubbing for hours and not being able to get up except to fetch more water. Some of the guards are cruel. They see us scrubbing the stone floors but keep walking through with their dirty boots, laughing and taunting. That's all right, I'll just picture I'm scrubbing their faces off. They're the dirt.

I try to work close to Emma when I can. There's one particular guard, Hadley, who torments her, kicks her, and is cruel, then takes her by the hand leading her away for a while, only to bring her back when he finishes with her.

"The swine," I whisper under my breath while nearly breaking my scrubbing brush on the stones.

Poor Emma doesn't have the heart to hate and fight. When he comes in with the rest of the guards, she hangs her head and keeps working, hoping he'll leave her alone. She doesn't deserve this. No one does.

Life here in the prison is uncertain. Not only do we have to put up with the guards who are more than cruel, but we also have to take caution around prisoners. Male and female. Many of the prisoners are hardened criminals who are dangerous. I see many are mind-crazy, driven mad from this life they have to suffer here in prison. Eventually some are sent to the gallows to be hanged. It's a horrid place.

With the prison so damp or wretchedly hot it causes everyone to be racked even more. It's unsanitary here. We're all crammed together where many are sick and diseased, making our every day agony. No wonder so many are crazy. At times I think, *Might I join them?*

There's one looney old woman by the name of Galda. She always walks around talking to herself. You don't dare get anywhere near her or turn your back on her if she's close. If she sees you looking at her and you move away, she'll grab you, ripping and tearing at you like an animal. She has no feeling for anyone. She'll attack for no reason and then leave you bleeding on the ground while she walks away talking to herself as if nothing's happened.

The guards never intervene when they see her battering someone. Don't think that they'll come to your rescue. So we've all learned to stay out of her way.

It's sad what made her this way. Galda has been here for many years. It's told that she saw her husband and children accidentally burn to death in a fire she had set in the house stove to keep warm. She had forgotten to secure the latch on the stove one night, and a log rolled out, starting a fire. She and her husband woke to the smell of smoke. Pushing her towards the door, he told her to run and get out of the house while he stayed inside to get their children. But they never came out. She had to listen to their screams and watch as their house burned with them inside. She never could deal with the fact that she had caused their deaths. Over time, her enormous grief twisted her mind as she was driven mad. Because she is such a danger to society, England sent her here.

At times I notice some guards are bothered with what happens here at the prison. I think those guards must be new to this land, fresh from Her Majesty's homeland. They're young, and are taught how to rape, abuse, and be cruel. In the beginning it must be torture for them, but soon they become hard-hearted, self-absorbed, and emotionless like the rest.

I try my best to stay away from all the guards, but life in prison doesn't give me many places where I can run and hide. Despite my best efforts to be good, I have a rebellious side that seems to get me into trouble. I guess I have to learn many of life's lessons the hard way. I hate being told what to do, or how to do it. That pushes me into stubbornness.

The guards and some of the women have little pity or patience with me. I hate the ugly men and dislike the old sows, but that's what I've become, fighting everything, and everyone. Maybe it's my age.

As I come back from work, minding my own business, two new women in our cell, Della and Janice, corner me.

"What are you doing?" I ask as they push me.

"Oh, we've come to teach you. You need guidance," says Della sarcastically.

Grabbing my clothes with one hand, and shoving a sharp stick under my chin with the other, she pins me to the wall.

"You need to learn, child," says Janice.

"You think you're something, but you ain't," snarls Della.

My heart pounds with fright, but I don't let on. Knowing I have my rusty knife tucked in my skirt waist, I glare back at them. But, why in the hell are they doing this? "Well, I killed a man," I say, hoping to scare them.

"Is that so?" she says, keeping her stick at my throat. "Well, so have I. You're a snip and don't know notin'," she snarls just inches from my nose.

"I killed someone too," Della tells me.

"We're tired of you around here. Tired of you making all that noise like you're someone," says Janice.

49

Too afraid to help, Emma and Liz watch from a distance as the two women push me around.

"You ain't nothin,' so stay with your young little group and keep your trap shut. Better know your place or we'll show you where that is, if you don't know.

"Who'd ya kill?" Della asks.

"My father," I answer, proudly standing in defiance.

"Well, I cut up my good-fer-nothin' husband, piece by piece, and fed 'em to the pigs," widening her eyes to scare me.

Janice stands close with a big grin on her face, wanting to fight.

"Well, dead is dead!" I bravely answer back, not backing down.

Shoving me harder against the wall, Della lets go and walks away, then quickly turns back around and snarls at me. "You just might find yourself dead if you keep it up, and none of us will care," she says.

Glaring at her, I watch as she slowly moves away.

Hurrying back to the safety of my friends, I plow my way past the crowd of girls who've been standing around watching.

Emma and Liz grab me and pull me to the bed.

"She's a bad one," says Liz.

Emma nods in agreement.

"You best stay clear of them," both my friends tell me.

Looking across the cell, my eyes follow the two hags as they go to their bunk. I don't know what I did to make them so angry. But I learnt a lesson today. I guess I'm not as important as I want to be.

"Who are they?" asks Emma.

"They're the new cows who came in on the last ship," I reply. "I guess they don't know who runs things around here."

Well, it ain't you," Emma says.

"I know."

"What might ya do about them?" asks Liz.

"Nothing right now, but I'll get 'em," I say glaring at them.

From talk in the cell, nobody likes them, but I'll wait. I'll think of something to get even.

About a week later, I ask Orla, "You still got that ladle you stole from the meal room?"

I know Liz has a loose stone in the wall by her bunk, so she and Orla hide things there.

Wide-eyed she stares at me, probably wondering how I know she has it. She looks at Liz, then back at me.

"Why?" she asks.

"I need it. Can I have it?"

"Sure," she says, pulling it from her hiding place.

"Make sure anything else you have is out of sight. The guards will probably do a check of the cell," I caution.

Those bitches are going to find out that things aren't easy around here. They've come into my world.

"Let's get em!" snickers Liz, looking at Orla and me.

※※※※※

Throughout the week the two new women argue with others, so they make my plan easier. They probably won't know who it is setting them up. *Me! That's who.* I'll wait for the perfect moment.

Some days later, I plant the ladle in their bunk, then go and whisper to Clarence, our guard on duty, telling him the new prisoners are hiding something in their bedding.

He nods, and walks over to another guard and shares the information. Everyone watches as the guards rip into their bed, finding the ladle. Grabbing the two hags, they drag them towards the cell door. Well, that's good for a lashing.

Our cell erupts with laughs and cheers as the guards take them away. They glare at everyone as they're led out. I hope they get the message. *We don't like you either.*

They're gone for now, but they'll be back and they won't be nice. But I don't care. All that matters is I got even. Don't get me wrong, many a time I've been on the other side of things. Sometimes I'm the one needing a lesson. So, I'm careful and watch them, and stay clear.

※※※※※

Coming in from work, Emma and I find someone has smashed shit all over our blankets. Pulling them off the bunk, we try to clean them the best we can, but still there's an awful stench. We're not the only ones that this has happened to. Almost every bunk, even Orla and Liz's, is covered with filth. This kind of thing happens often when someone gets mad.

Looking around, I see others trying to clean their beds. We all know who did it. It's Della and Janice, the two I snitched on. Noticing the smirk on their faces, I don't react or give them the satisfaction that I know they did it.

"It's all your fault!" Emma whispers angrily.

"What do you mean?" I snap back.

Looking around to make sure no one else is listening, she says, "You make everyone mad, and no one likes you, Adeleen. I don't think I like you anymore, either."

Looking at Emma, I see tears welling up in her eyes. I know she's right. I make a lot of enemies, and very few friends.

"Things will change," I tell her.

"Well, I don't believe you."

I have to change, or I'll lose my best friend.

"I'll try to be better, I promise, I'll really try," I say.

Emma looks at me with disgust then walks over to where Liz and Orla are sitting in their bunk. With my three friends looking at me, I feel ashamed. I walk over quietly to sit with them as their soiled blankets lie on the floor.

It takes a week for the foul smell to go away. I hate what I've become in this place.

12

I hear her screams as I see guard Hadley grab Emma's hair, pulling her across the floor. He begins kneeing and hitting her in her face. Water from her bucket spills everywhere as he flings her around like a rag doll.

Emma puts up her hands to deflect his blows, but he's too strong. I see her blood splatter everywhere. Why is he so angry with her? Then his final kick is to her head, and she slumps to the floor. Emma must have gotten in his way, and he has just unleashed his anger on her.

I risk everything and run to her, only to be shoved away by the other guards. I'm lost and don't know what to do.

The guards stand around talking, then nudge at her with their boots to see if she moves.

Do something! I silently scream within myself. My heart pounds almost out of my chest from witnessing the attack, but I don't dare move. Finally one guard picks Emma up, cradling her in his arms, carrying her out the door towards the hospital.

EMMA!

We're told never go over to the Fever Hospital unless we're ordered, so I don't know anything about it. I see the building in the distance, and my mind races trying to plot what to do. My anger wells within me as my hatred for the guards grows.

The other girls and I rush to the water trough where we can whisper about what just happened while we fill our pails. Nobody knows what to do. We're all shaken and afraid.

"Is she dead?" asks one girl.

"I don't know," I whisper, "but I'm going to find out."

"How?" another asks.

"I'll find a way, just keep working."

The fear on everyone's faces says it all. We know what can happen if we don't get back to work, so we must all hurry. One guard keeps watching us, then yells, "Get back to work, you ugly bitches, or you're next!"

Fearful, we scurry back to where we were working. I keep my head down, not looking at any of them in fear the same will happen to me. Going over to where Emma's blood is splattered on the floor, I begin to wipe it up. My heart hurts, but I can't cry. The guards wouldn't let me.

It has been two days now, and Emma still hasn't come back to our cell. How badly is she hurt? My mind reels, and I can't rest worrying about her.

Finally, a thought comes to me. A way to go find her, if she's still at the hospital. But, I'll need help from the women.

Occasionally, when we finish the floors, we're allowed to wash at the pump. Staying fully dressed, we're allowed to douse ourselves with the left-over buckets of soapy water and scrub our stinking bodies and dresses at the same time.

So, today I ask the girls when they're finished with work, to go over to the pump and start washing themselves. Even though it's getting colder outside, I tell the girls to try to look like their enjoying it. I know the guards won't be able to take their eyes from them, and I can sneak away to the hospital. I hope I can find Emma. I need to at least try. God willing, I'll be heading that way.

There! We've finished the floors and the girls head over to the pump. Like we planned, they start bathing. The guards can't resist the girls laughing and teasing so, unnoticed, I walk towards the hospital building. Finally I'm out of the guards' sight, but still carrying my pail to look like I'm supposed to be going there for work. No one even suspects anything. Stupid guards!

Then, I'm at the hospital door. Opening it, I step inside. Putting down the pail of water, I look around the room. There are so many beds with poor souls laying in them. How do I find Emma? I see two young women talking, but they're unaware I've slipped in. They have blood all over the front of their belly aprons. I'm sure it's not their blood because they don't look hurt.

Where is she? Where's my Emma? One by one I look at the helpless in each bed, many who are groaning from pain. The women are busy trying to help and give comfort to those they can.

Then, I spot her. Rushing to her side, I fall on the floor beside her bed.

"Oh, Emma," I whisper, taking her hand

She doesn't hear me, so I shake her a little, and whisper her name in her ear.

"Emma, Emma, it's me, Adeleen," I whisper a little louder.

Nothing! She doesn't even move her eyes.

Just how hurt are you? Why aren't you getting any better?

"Emma, wake up, I need you. Please wake up, oh God, please wake up, Emma," I plead louder as tears run down my face.

One of the women catches sight of me and comes running over. "You're not supposed to be here. You need to go before they find you," she warns me.

"What's wrong with her?" I ask.

"The doctor says she's in a coma and probably won't live."

Those are the words I can't bear to hear. Feeling desperate and crying, I put my face close to Emma's.

"Please don't die. I don't want to be here alone. Please don't die. This is hell, and I don't want to be here alone. Emma!" Tears running off my face onto her cheek.

I put my hand on her stomach to see if I can feel her baby. A baby she felt move for the first time only days ago. But nothing, it too lies quiet. Then I feel a hand on my shoulder. It's the young woman trying to pull me to my feet.

"You must leave, it's too dangerous for you to be here," she whispers.

"Don't you understand? I can't leave her. She needs me," I plead.

Suddenly there are loud voices coming from down the hall. Fearing the worst, the girl tells me, "It's the doctor. Quick, lie flat, and slide under the bed…hurry!"

Hidden safely beneath Emma's bed, I hear him enter the room. I can only see the lower part of his trousers and boots as he walks around pausing for a moment at each bed. Quickly the girl pulls the blanket, and drapes it to hide me.

Stopping at Emma's bed, he asks, "How's she doing today?"

Inches away from my face are his finely polished black boots. Eager to hear what he is going to do to help Emma, I lie still and listen.

"There's no change, Doctor," she replies.

He grunts then walks on.

Angry, I find myself wanting to jump out from under the bed and grab him, but instead I stay quiet with hate welling up inside. *You bastard, do something. What kind of doctor are you?*

After he leaves the room, I scoot out from under the bed. "How can I get a job here?" I ask her frantically.

"I don't know. He just grabbed me one day, brought me here, and told me to take care of the sick. At first I couldn't stand all the blood, sickness, and death, but over time I got used to it. All I know is, I don't want to be one of them," she says as she sadly looks at Emma.

I have to find a way to work here. It's Emma's and my only hope.

"Who grabbed you?" I ask.

"It was Doctor Ross, who you heard while you were under the bed."

"I didn't see his face. Where did he go?"

"To the next building. That's where he lives. If you hurry to the window, you'll see him. He's tall, with dark hair and a beard. He's the one in the black suit."

Hurrying to the window I see him walk across the yard. Narrowing my eyes on him, I vow, *somehow I'll get a job here.*

Before rushing out, I turn. "I don't know your name."

"It's Mary."

"I'm Adeleen. Thanks for helping, Mary."

Grabbing my pail, I stop to look back at Emma, then dart out the door.

When I return to my cell, I find they have already put someone else in Emma's spot in my bunk. I don't care, so I just ignore her. I can't sleep thinking about Emma. It's storming again, and the dampness runs down the cold stone walls. Wrapping myself in my blanket, I kick at my new bunkmate to make her move to give me more room. Restless, while listening to the coughing from the sick women in my cell, I try to think of a way to help Emma.

That's it!

Jumping to my feet, I go to the sickest girl. "Get up and come with me. I'll take you to the doctor." I feel bad because she's so weak and can barely stand. Throwing her arm over my shoulder, I practically have to carry her.

I yell for Morry, the night guard, and I tell him how sick she is and that I must take her to the hospital. Hoping he will say yes, I stand holding her and waiting for him to make a decision. Then she coughs in his face, and he quickly unlocks the iron door and waves us out.

"You get over there straight away, and no place else."

Letting us go alone isn't supposed to happen, but I know he'll be with Liz tonight and she'll keep his mind on other things. He probably won't even remember we're gone. Besides, I lied to him. I'm not going to the hospital, but to the doctor's house.

Blowing in off the ocean, a cold, icy rain from a winter storm has arrived. Even though I try to hurry, our clothes become soaked by the time we reach the doctor's door. I knock, but no one can hear because of the pouring rain, so I pound even louder. They should hear me now.

Then I hear the lock turn as an old woman slowly opens the door.

I tell her, "She's deathly sick, and I was told to bring her to the doctor."

The old housemaid thinks for a moment, then motions for us to come inside out of the rain. Pointing to a chair, she nods for us to go sit.

Taking the girl over, I sit her down and stand beside her. "I don't even know your name," I whisper.

"Clara," she says as she struggles to breathe.

Soon the doctor appears from another room. "What are you doing here?"

Almost afraid of him, for a moment I'm left speechless. Then, "She's sick with great fever. The guard told me to bring her here."

"Those damn guards, they never follow directions," he grumbles.

He puts the back of his hand to Clara's forehead and then motions to the old woman. "Get her out of here. Take her over to the hospital with the rest of the sick. She can die there."

Glaring at him, *what a cold-hearted bastard you are.*

"You, you need to stay," says the doctor pointing at me. "I need more help in the hospital."

Just like that, I have a new job.

The old woman and I take Clara over to the hospital. Then I follow her back to the house where she shows me to a room with an empty bed. She motions and tells me, "This is where you can stay for tonight, but tomorrow we'll find you a bed at the hospital."

Standing, and looking in the room, I see a real bed, with a mattress, pillow, and blanket.

I never see Clara again. Sadly, I heard she died that same night. I wish I had told her, "Thank you." She never knew how she helped me.

❦❦❦❦❦

It's only been one day since I've started helping in the hospital. For me to see Emma lie unconscious is hard. She's my best friend in this whole world. What can I do to get her well?

Looking around at the other patients, I feel disgusted at the suffering they have to endure. I try to give each one comfort, if nothing more than a drink of water, or a word of encouragement. But other than that, there's nothing much I can do, except to clean up after them.

Some patients scream and moan in agonizing pain more than others. They've had amputations or broken bones set. Others lie crying, and some, like Emma, remain quiet. The old are merely brought here to die. The guards would rather send them here than deal with them, they're too much trouble.

58

From across the room, I notice Emma's breathing begins to slow, and it's then I realize she's going to die.

My heart breaks because there's nothing I can do to save her. I try to give her water, but she's unable to swallow. Her tongue has already begun to swell from the slow process from not drinking. Still, I won't give up. I put a damp cloth to her lips, looking for some spark of life. Does she even know I'm with her?

"I'll make Hadley pay, Emma," I whisper in her ear. "I'll make that bastard pay for what he's done to you. Somehow, some way, he'll suffer for this, I promise you."

I can't stay by her bed too long, or the doctor will know why I'm here. So I tend to the others close by her but always keep one eye on my friend. I'm never far away. Late afternoon, I glance over her direction and notice her breathing has almost stopped.

Quickly I run to her side. Holding her hand, I watch as she takes her last breath. My heart races, as if it's trying to beat for her.

"No! I don't want you to go! Emma!" Crying, I put my cheek next to hers. "Emma, please don't go!" I whisper in agony.

A gentle breeze blows in off the ocean. I reach out my hand so it brushes hers as two men take her body away. They carry Emma out past the iron gates, leading somewhere far away from the prison, to an unmarked common grave out in the desert.

The guards won't allow me to go, but at least I was by her side when she died. Out beyond the walls, Emma and her unborn baby will rest, overlooking the blue waters of the vast ocean. Maybe now she will have peace.

Another hole in my heart is left to fill with emptiness. I wrestle with the question, why am I still alive?

Looking out in the direction they've taken her, I vow, I'd rather be dead than live the rest of my life in this prison. My struggles will not stop me. Even though I'm beaten down, I will only get stronger. No matter how long it takes, I will find a way out of this hell and be free of this vile place.

13

There are only a few male prisoners working at the hospital. They bring in the injured and dying, or take away the dead. I've often seen the two men who carried Emma away after she died. Each day they come in to see if any of us need help lifting any of the patients. They look ragged, but I sense their good hearts by the gentle way they respect and treat the sick and dead. I don't know their names yet, but they smile and nod each time I see them.

Women are to have very little conversation with the men prisoners. I'm not supposed to speak to any of the helpers, the guards make sure of that. They want to keep the women for themselves.

But, working here at the hospital, I do feel safer. The guards don't have such easy access to me, and that's a good thing.

It's not long and I find out the names of the two men. Sometimes these hardworking men bring supplies to the kitchen. Lifting heavy supplies they never complain. Approaching the older of the two, I dare to strike up a conversation.

"My name is Adeleen. I want to thank you for your help."

Nodding, he greets me with a deep voice and a strange accent. "You're welcome, mademoiselle. My name is Mychael and this young man is Louie."

Looking over at Louie, he smiles, then bends at his waist. Oh my, such gentlemen they both are. Louie is much younger than Mychael, maybe sixteen years old, or so. He's missing most of his front teeth, but he's still cute when he smiles. Mychael, on the other hand, is older. He's a Frenchman, polite, curly dark hair, and very fine-looking, I must say. I think I feel my toes curling. Anyway, we all stay quiet and keep to ourselves and speak only if spoken to, which is the way it's supposed to be.

❦❦❦❦❦❦

My working at the hospital gives me freedom to come and go as needed. Often times, I'm sent to retrieve the so-called doctor. Doctor Ross, they call him. How can they call him a doctor? I've never seen him doctor anyone. All he does is look at the patients and grunt.

It's not long before Doctor Ross takes a liking to me and summons me to his bed. When he finishes at the hospital, he tells me to follow him. The other girls watch as we leave. They understand he's chosen me for tonight; he's already had his turn with each of them.

The first time I walk into his bedroom, I notice a bath is waiting. Moving behind a dressing screen, he disrobes.

"When I'm finished bathing, you need to bathe," he says. "You smell."

"Yes, sir," I answer. *What do you expect? I haven't had a real bath since I was pushed in the ocean years ago.*

Turning away, I don't watch as he gets into his tub.

"You may wash my back, and not too hard," he orders.

"Yes, sir."

Hiding my disgust, I reach for a cloth. He's boney. Not much fat on his puny body. The stress of being a good-for-nothing doctor must wear on him. It doesn't take long, and soon he steps out of his bath and robes himself. Standing in front of a mirror, he picks up small comb and grooms his beard.

"Pour me a drink," he demands, pointing to a small table against the wall.

Hurrying over, I see beautiful crystal glasses and liquor bottles are neatly placed. *Well, he's well supplied.* Handing him his drink as he sits in a chair on the other side of the room, where he'll have a clear view of the tub.

"You may bathe now," he says, staring at me.

I take a deep breath and begin to undress. Running through my mind, I try to think of good things about all this is. I get a bath, and he keeps himself clean and doesn't have the stench like the guards. Is it worth it all? I'll see.

Over the evening, I see him drink heavily. I don't like this man, but I don't have a choice. Hell, I've never liked any of them. Maybe when he's not watching, I can sneak a sip of his drink, it might help me to endure him.

❦❦❦❦❦

I've been taken to his bed for a month now, and he's never asked my name. I keep silent while in his presence, not wanting to talk to him. Sometimes I think I make him somewhat nervous. He sees me watching him and starts fidgeting. He's hungry for a woman; it is evident by the way he violently covers my body. I feel the agony within his every move. He's angry but still craving for a woman, and wanting only that release that will give him comfort. That's all. He keeps his feelings closed, but I feel the emotional wall he has built up. A wall he thinks protects him, but sadly, it only makes him cold within.

The doctor is so concerned with his cleanliness at times he seems to make himself crazy. I notice after he leaves the hospital the blood on his clothing bothers him, even though he cuts off limbs and operates even when there's no reason. When he gets to his residence, he is so obsessed with ridding himself of the blood-stained clothes, he makes sure his housekeeper removes them, sending them to be cleaned as soon as possible. Then he takes his bath.

I hate being his property, but I know that I'm better off than most girls. There are times when passion will run through my body, and I try my best to suppress it, but I'm a woman now and so desire the touch of a man, even a man I despise. But still, I live with fear. I know it will only be a matter of time before he too will tire of me and throw me aside like all the rest. What an ugly life.

❦❦❦❦❦

Today at the hospital, I hear girls talking about a prison break. Rumors are always going around. Someone is always planning an escape, so I keep my ears open for an opportunity I might want to try. It's frightening though. Sometimes the escapees disappear, but later the guards tell us they perished in the desert. We never know for sure if they made it or not.

I think this attempt is doomed to fail. There are too many who know about it, and that's dangerous. I notice the guards are watching more carefully what everyone is doing. That's a sure sign they suspect something's up.

Marie, one of the girls helping in the kitchen, tells me, "The guards found some weapons missing from their armory."

"How do you know?"

"I heard them talking about it while they were eating."

Sure enough, the guards start searching the men's cells. It won't take long for them to find out who's planning it. They have their ways of making someone talk.

"There are five men who plan to make a break."

"Who told you this?"

"Oh, I overheard Milly telling Laura. She knows everything that goes on around here. The men plan to go tonight and shoot their way out if they have to."

Looking at the guards standing around, I know this break is one I don't want to be a part of. These men are going to find themselves shot dead or on the end of a rope if they don't make it.

And sure enough, someone snitches. Before long, they have all five men in chains. Not even a shot is fired.

So much for their plans. I knew they wouldn't get away with it.

Now the guards make us prisoners gather in the hot sun to witness the five men as they force them up the steps of the gallows. Standing beside Liz and Orla, I remain silent. It gives me plenty to think about. *Do I dare try?*

The noise of the trap doors slams, and I gasp as they drop. It's a gruesome sight as they dance upon nothing.

"Do you know any of them?" I ask the girls.

"No, I think they haven't been here very long. It's clear they don't know that you never get out of here," says Liz.

We'll see about that...I will someday.

I think it's been eight years since I've come to this hell. As I grow older, I have learned how to live in the most horrible conditions, and still, somehow, I find some peace among these hard, stone walls.

I've come to the realization my life isn't going to be anything other than what it is as long as I stay here. For now, I learn to accept my life and quit fighting everything so much. Over time, I even earn the right to work unsupervised. Pushing back against everything has only brought me more trouble.

Maybe this understanding comes with my age or that knowing nothing I do will change a thing. Still, late at night, I hear the muffled screams of human pain that enshrouds this place. But those sounds too, I have learned to block out. It just happens.

Often girls come back to their cells with blackened eyes, and I know. But at least this time, it's not me. With this acceptance, I become obedient and do what I'm told.

I'm always keeping my eyes open for my way of escape, though. I have no plans, but until then, I'll be good.

Many times I've tried to take keys that unlock the gates. Then I rethink. Where do I go? How will I eat? If I were to go out of the gate without permission and make my way towards the village, the guards would surely find me. So for now, I keep my eyes and ears open for something else.

I know other eyes are watching for escape too, eyes that I can trust. Louie is always telling me about rumors. He's young and doesn't seem to know when to keep his mouth shut. I've seen Mychael give Louie the eye when he blabs too much. Mychael knows I will try someday. He only has a ten-year sentence, so all he has to do is his time. He won't risk it.

I spend my time helping in the hospital, and other times in the kitchen, or wherever they need me the most. Sometimes both jobs on the same day. I'm just thankful I don't have to scrub floors any longer. I don't mind, I get to be around more women, and that's what we need — each other. They're the closest I have to family.

A guard brings an injured female into the hospital care room. Another prisoner has thrown a rock, hitting her in the face. I gasp when I see her. She's wearing Emma's dress. I remember the dress — it's grey and has tiny blue flowers scattered over it. No one else in prison has a dress like it. It's one of the prettiest.

Staring at her for a moment, I bring myself back to task and grab a cloth, putting pressure on the gash across her forehead. Seeing the blood running down her face and neck onto the front of the dress, I close my eyes for a second and shudder. I remember how we get our clothes.

"This here's our little darkie, Rou," says the guard. "She needs some sewin', so stitch her pretty," he chuckles.

Doctor Ross comes into the room, moves forward, and takes the bloody cloth from my hand. Stepping back, I watch as he sutures the gash on her forehead. She's so brave. She sits quietly on the table, letting him stitch her wound while only making a kind of humming sound. When he finishes, he tells her to stand. She's a tall, slender African girl with dark skin that shimmers from drops of sweat on her body.

The guard and I watch as the doctor removes the dress from off her shoulders, dropping it to her waist. As he slowly looks over her body, I see he's aroused and taken in by her raw beauty. He stands there for a moment, then takes her by her waist and turns her around until she's facing away from him. Pressing against her, he tilts her over the table and slowly runs his hands down her scarred back; one that shows she's been whipped many times. She rolls her eyes in disgust, but doesn't resist and stands in submission. Then, the moment passes as he seems to pull himself out of the trance he's in. Grabbing her dress, he lifts it back onto her shoulders. Without saying a word, he motions for the guard to take her out, and then he walks through a doorway into another room. As Rou passes me, she looks straight into my eyes and I understand.

65

After work that day, the doctor tells me I won't be needed at his residence tonight. Well, that's a relief. Sadly, I'll miss my bath though. Walking back to my cell, I'm told by the girls that he's summoned Rou to his bed. Poor girl.

A week later I see Rou taking something to wash. She smiles when she sees me.

"Hello. Do you remember me?" I ask.

"Yes, I sure do," Rou answers with a heavy accent.

"How's your head?" I ask looking at her wound.

"It no bother me."

"I hear you spend the nights with the doctor."

"Mmmhmm. He's trouble, this man," she says.

"I know, I've been to his bed too.

"You sure can have 'im back, I don't want 'im," she says.

Laughing, I shake my head, "No, no, you keep him. I don't want him either."

We both laugh.

Looking around and being careful the guards don't notice us talking too much, I get nosy and continue questioning her.

"Why do they call you Rou?"

"No one's able to say me real name, so dey call me, Rou. Sometimes I don't know for sure if I remember. It's been a long time since anyone say me real name. I sure do wish someone would say it, though. I miss hearing it."

"You can teach it to me. I'll try to say it for you."

"Maybe's I can teach you."

"What brought you to the prison?" I ask.

"I don' know, I just been sent here. That's how's it is with us dark ones. 'Ever I go, they don' say, they just do."

I remember in England seeing people like her, but I knew little about where they came from. But of course, I was young and didn't know much anyway.

"I'd better go Rou. We'll talk another time."

"Yes, dat be fine," she tells me with a smile.

Over time, Rou and I get to know each other better. Even though she's with the doctor every night, we see each other almost daily. Like

66

me, she is sent to work in the kitchen, and we soon become good friends.

She has a mischievous side and tells me the things she does to confuse the doctor. Maybe pull threads on the seams of his trousers so they will soon unravel, or loosen a button, causing them to eventually fall off. And better yet, she snips a piece of yarn in his socks so that holes will open. Knowing the doctor, it's probably driving him crazy. She's a clever girl, and I like her. Why not? I think she's a lot like me — she wants to get even.

14

It's winter again in the Australian desert. Extra help is needed in the kitchen today, my favorite place to work. It's always warm by the stove, and they make sure to keep the eating room warm for the guards.

Looking out the window across the desert, I see puddles left from the rain. The dampness from the storm is making prisoners sick again. The guards have a small stove they huddle around, but it's not close enough to warm our cells. I just have my one blanket and sometimes that's not enough. I'm glad there's someone in my bunk with me, we can huddle together for extra warmth.

This time of year the wet winds never seem to stop blowing, drenching everything in their path. My nights are the coldest, especially if I've been out in the rain, and I have no way to get dry. I'm always glad to see the sun come up, giving what little warmth it does. I've heard that desert land is supposed to be hot but that's not true in the winter, especially after the sun disappears. No wonder everything has a hard time trying to stay alive.

This harsh, barren land has a real chill this morning as I walk to the kitchen. I look to the corner of the yard and see a young desert hopper scratching around for something to eat.

"You'd better run, little one. This prison is no place to make your home. Go back through the gate, go out and find something to eat away from here. If you stay, they'll gather you up for the stew pot," I whisper to him.

Walking into the kitchen, I'm glad to be here today. Lifting a large pot onto the stove gives me a chance to warm up, and dry off. This is one of the best jobs to have in the winter. But I still miss the fresh air from the long walks in the desert.

It becomes loud as the guards enter the meal room. Those bastards. *It's feeding time for the rats.* Out the kitchen window, I see more guards coming in to eat. I keep my eye on Hadley, the guard who killed Emma. No one likes him, not even the other guards. He's repulsive and one of the cruelest. Rou and I are the cooks today, so no telling what we'll put in his meal.

Yukiya and Sarah have to dish up the food. But then there are the other poor women who pour drinks for the guards. They have to endure the grabs and the jeers daily. I hear the guards taunting them and see how cruel a room full of vulgar, ugly men can be.

❦❦❦❦

It's my birthday today. Well, not really. We girls all have picked a time when we want to celebrate our birthdays. It gives us some happiness and something to look forward to. I don't really know when mine is exactly, and I'm not sure even how old I am. I think I'm twenty now. I've lost count of how long I've been here. I know when I see the full moon move across the sky and it touches a particular mountain out in the desert, it's another year, and I celebrate my birthday. One of the other women showed me that trick. Not that it makes any difference.

A few of them remember it and give me small gifts throughout my day. There's a flower picked from one of the weeds outside. I smell its sweet fragrance and remember there's still something beautiful about this world. Then there are a few small seashells from the ocean. How they got them, I don't ask.

But my eyes widen as I see a small comb for my hair. It's crudely hand-carved from an old piece of blue wood that must have drifted with the currents and found its way to the Australian shore. Who would make such a thing for me? I hope the guards don't take it because I can do so much damage to someone's face with it. They're stupid though and probably won't think about it.

"It's from Mychael. He slipped it to me and told me to give it to you for your birthday," says Millie.

"It's so beautiful."

"You be lucky, Adeleen. Men like you. I wish they would look at me the way they look at you," she says.

I look at her and wish she could read my thoughts. *So they can rape you more than others? You don't know what you're wishing for. Most men are attracted to me. Sometimes the guards fight over me, but that sickens me.*

Shaking my head as if it's nothing, I look at the comb and am curious how he was able to carve it. What happened to bring Mychael to this ugly prison? Pulling my long, red hair up on top of my head, I quickly tuck it into my unruly locks. The comb is perfect.

Working in the kitchen gives me an opportunity to talk freely with Mychael and Louie. During a moment when they're bringing in supplies, I ask about any escape rumors at the prison. Mychael and Louie both shake their heads that they haven't heard of any.

Smiling at Mychael, I whisper, "Thank you for the beautiful comb."

He smiles, nods, and whispers back, *"Joyeux anniversaire, Mademoiselle Adeleen."* As they go to walk out, Louie looks back with a big grin.

French, he's speaking French to me. I don't know what he said, but I think it might be 'Happy birthday.' I again give a slight smile and nod to them both.

❦❦❦❦❦

It's my day to milk the cows with Rou. As we walk to the barn we hear a scuffle. Two prisoners are in a fight. The guards look on, not eager to pull them apart. They enjoy watching them pound on each other. There's no sympathy ever given from any of the guards for anyone.

Often the male prisoners will fight to exhaustion or near death. There's plenty of hate and rage built up in these caged-up men. Sooner or later it just has to erupt. I guess the guards' think it's better the prisoners hit each other rather than them.

When the men are finished fighting, the guards will take them for a lashing, and sometimes not. It depends on the mood of the guards or how badly the men are beat up.

I don't want to watch, so I look away. I'm sick of all the fighting.

Rou and I walk into the barn to where the cows are waiting to be milked.

"Well, hello, fat cow, you got any milk for me today?" I ask as I walk up, taking the stool to sit on.

Rou laughs, and says to her cow, with her African accent, "Yeah, you'd bedder give us some milk, missy cow, or else we'll get whipped. So you come on, you pretty cow, you fill my pail."

I listen as Rou begins to hum a tune, filling the barn with a rare moment of peace.

Sitting on my stool, I look to the barnyard where some men are trying to corner a young bull to castrate. Even getting close to the young bull is a real effort, let alone trying to put a rope around its horns.

Rou and I laugh as we watch the young bull kick at them, tossing one of the men through the air with its horns. But sadly, they're able to hobble the animal's legs, rendering it helpless. Pulling the bull into the stall, they have him secure, although its strength's a real match for them.

I want to watch. I've heard about castration, but I've never seen it done. I hold my breath as the bull bellows with pain. It takes only a few minutes, and then it's over. He sure is mad when they let him loose.

"Hell, they need to castrate d'emselves. D'em all needs to be cut, far as I like. No evil man needs 'em," she says while looking at me with her dark eyes. The big grin on her face makes me chuckle.

Milking my cow, stroking her soft hide, I lay my cheek against her warmth, lost in my thoughts. Quietly, I think about my life and realize I need to quit feeling sorry for myself and find some way out of this prison.

Rou finishes and is putting back her stool when her cow spreads its hind legs wide apart to pee. I watch as Rou quickly grabs a small pot she has tied to her belt cord and captures what she can.

"Bloody hell! Rou, what are you doing?"

"Oh, 'tisn't nutten," she says as I watch her pour the pee into her pail of milk.

I laugh and shake my head.

Picking up her pail, Rou smiles and says, "I must go, the guards needs 'der milk."

Smiling, I turn to milk my cow and take extra time stroking and talking to her. I don't want to go back, but I know I have to. If I take too long, then next time they'll tell someone else to go milk. So I hurry and finish.

⁂

I now alternate weekly with another women to take a bucket of water to the guards' station high up on the wall for them to drink. From there I can look down and see another transport ship unloading prisoners in the cove. The wagons bring them from the shore to the prison, and then they are herded into the holding yard.

Today, I can't believe what I'm seeing. My eyes narrow on him, watching him move in line with the other prisoners. It's been a lot of years, but is it him? Am I sure? Yes, I am.

He's the man who worked for my father and helped hunt me down. He was one of the two men responsible for dragging my mum from the house that awful day. He's the one who pulled the curtain back and found me hiding, grabbing my dress, tearing it as I climbed through the window running from the house. And he's the one who found me in the shed. Why is he here? Must have been up to no good, that's for sure.

My thoughts reel. Now I have a real purpose in my life. Somehow, I will get to him. I will go to the ends of the earth to make his life hell. Like a spider in its web, this prison is my place. I have nothing but time. His hell will be even greater, I will see to it.

I remember his face. His was the first face I learned to carve into my memory and hate. I was just nine years old when he last saw me, so I don't think he'll recognize me. I'm almost sure of that. It can't be more perfect.

Two days later, as usual, I take the water up to the guards for them to drink. This afternoon is extra hot, so I know they need fresh water by now.

Standing on the wall, I can see down on the new prisoners. The young girls huddle over in the corner of the yard, and I know they will soon be led through the wooden door to the small yard to wait. My heart goes out to them, for I remember what will happen to them before the night is over. Sadly, they're not my focus for today.

I look across the yard at the crowd of prisoners and spot him again. He isn't going anywhere for a while, that's for sure. I'm going to need time to figure something out.

Tonight it's hard for me to sleep. My mind races to plot all the things I can do to make his life pure hell. I know I will have plenty of time for planning, but for now, I let myself imagine.

❧❧❧❧❧

I stand back watching as guards roughly bring another prisoner into the care room. It takes two guards to hold this one upright. He's been lashed at the post for God knows what, but mostly for being a loudmouth troublemaker.

Everyone calls him "Asa," although I don't know if that's his real name. But that's what the guards call him. He's been here many times. He makes his life difficult for himself but seems to take pleasure in that, which is hard to understand.

"Clean 'em up, and don't dally!" a guard yells as they shove him towards the table.

Unsteady on his feet, he appears to be intoxicated. But he isn't, he's just had the hell beat out of him, that's all.

Asa chuckles loudly and then smiles as he struggles to keep his balance.

Taking his arm I guide him to the table.

73

"Hi, little lady," he says, winking.

"Shhh," I whisper. "You'll make things worse."

"Ahh, it can't get no worse," he chuckles. "You're looking pretty today. How you able to stay so pretty in this ugly hell hole?" Wiping the blood from his wounds, he flinches.

"Why do you keep doing this to yourself?" I sadly ask.

"Oh, it ain't nothing. They just need to show me they don't like me," he says, taunting the guards with a leer.

"Hurry up!" the guard snaps.

Once the wounds stop bleeding, they grab him and push him towards the door. As they do, he smiles at me again. "See you next time, pretty little lady."

Lieutenant Samuel, a British officer assigned to the prison who's been somewhat friendly towards me, becomes aware of what I must be thinking about how Asa is being treated.

The Lieutenant lingers after the guard takes him out. "Asa's a troublemaker, you know."

"I know," I reply as I watch the guards roughly take him away. "I guess that's how he copes. Maybe he needs to feel a greater pain than what's inside him. I understand him."

Just then, Sara comes into the room. "Hurry, the doctor needs our help," she says.

"I'll be right there."

I leave Lieutenant Samuel standing there, and then look back. "This is all we know," I say, walking away.

❦❦❦❦❦

My friends and I have fun while making the guards lives a little miserable. At night we sit in our bunks plotting what mischief we can do to them. I must say, it puts some fun in living in this rat hole and gives us some enjoyment when one of us succeeds. But we also shudder when one of us gets caught and has to be lashed, or even worse, when guards take out their anger in other ways.

Unknown to the guards, we tamper with their things, or we try to confuse them. We're willing to take the risk of getting caught, but who cares? We get beaten plenty of times anyway.

This afternoon one of the girls has stuffed something down the guard's privy so they'd have nowhere to relieve themselves except to come over to the prisoners' smelly stench hole, something they hate to do.

From out of the privy, Orla and I hear a guard shouting and cursing. Quickly we hurry away from the door because we know he'll be coming out angry. Exiting he's damning the whole world as he looks down at the mess on his boots. We're far enough away and snicker. The only problem is we're the ones who will clean it up. But what the hell? We get a laugh out of it.

I've learned how to carefully catch spiders, or pincer insects, to torment the guards. I put them in their folded uniforms, or other various places we know the guards will be. Then later we hear them swearing as they kill them.

Once, I even killed a rat in the kitchen and knew just what I wanted to do with it. The only problem is I had to carry the dead thing in my pocket for two days. I knew I would have my opportunity to put it in one of their boots. If not, it would be just ripe enough for their stew.

We don't always get to see the results of our mischief, but sometimes I'm close enough to hear the guards cussing. That's when I know we've done our job well. It feels good to laugh.

It doesn't take long before the guards get wise to us, and start grabbing one of us whenever something happens. I think they grab Rou more often. They seem to pick on her. But Rou doesn't let them break her spirit. I look up to her for that. She'd been through a lot in her life.

15

Finally, it's the last day the new prisoners will be held in the yard. I have to make my move now.

Millie gets the pail ready to take fresh water up to the guards' station on the wall. I stop her. "I'll do that today," I tell her as I pull the pail from her hands. Looking at me confused, she reluctantly lets go.

Carrying the heavy bucket over to the wall, I look up and see the thirsty guards standing in the scorching sun. Taking a deep breath, *It's now or never.* I step on the first rung of the ladder and begin my climb.

"Adeleen, where've you been?" grumbles a guard, Edwards. "You're late! Next time get here sooner. It's hot up here."

"Ah, don't bark at her, she's fine," says another guard, Reeves, as he smiles at me and dips the ladle into the fresh water.

From up here there's a clear view of all the prisoners. Quickly scanning the male prisoners, I try to figure out which one is the most dangerous in the group. It doesn't take long before I spot him. He's the biggest, meanest looking man down there. He's the one to be reckoned with. I nod to myself. *He'll do.*

I know the routine. The men have been kept separate from the women in in a different yard. They've been there a week now. Why? I don't know. Maybe the guards like to let them bake for a while in the hot Australian sun.

My plan has to be timed right for it to work. It will be risky for me to get close to the new prisoners, so I'll have to be quick.

With a clear view of the yard, I see my opportunity. I notice a guard walking along the fence. I wager he's thirsty. All I have to do is wait for him to turn and walk the other way. The guards above probably won't see me since they're usually talking to each other and not paying attention.

Slowly I climb down the ladder, then walk along the fence close to the prisoners. The giant brute of a man is standing near enough he should be able to hear me. Holding my breath, I quickly move closer. Let's hope he has good hearing.

"Hey, you!"

Startled, he looks at me.

"See that fellow over there with his back to you? He's telling everyone you ain't nothing, and when the time is right he'll mash your face, then make you his woman."

I watch his eyes narrow and can see the fight swelling up inside him as his feet pound the ground, stomping across the yard straight at my target.

Suddenly, the guard walks back in my direction and spots me.

"Hey, get away! What the hell you think you're doing over there?" he yells.

"Nothing," I answer. Pointing to the guards high on the wall, I tell him, "After I finished up top, I thought you might be thirsty too. But that big man wants me to give him some water. I told him, 'No!' This water's for the guards only."

Nodding, he takes the ladle and drinks. As I watch out of the corner of my eye, the big fellow walks over and taps my target on his shoulder. When he turns, the man punches him right in the face. *Ha, how's that feel? Do it again,* I want to yell.

Hearing the commotion, the guard drops the ladle and walks towards the fence to see what's happening.

Rushing to the ladder, I climb halfway up to see better.

One of the guards sees me and yells, "Move along, Adeleen. Get down off the ladder!"

Slowly I climb down, all the while watching my target getting beat. I can't stay and watch, but that's fine, I don't need to. I know what's happening, and what else will happen.

I take the pail back to the kitchen and quickly hand it to Millie. "I'm late for the hospital. I have to hurry." Rushing out through the door, I'm excited to go to my next job.

I put on my hospital belly apron and start helping the prisoners who need treatment. All the while I'm laughing inside. Very soon, I know my target will be one that guards drag in through the door. I can hardly wait.

About an hour later, the door slams open as the guards bring in both men. Yep, there he is. All beat up and not walking so straight.

I know that when the new prisoners are in a fight the guards take them to be lashed. They tie them to a post in the yard for all to see as they're whipped. It's meant to be a deterrent for those who want to fight. But it doesn't work...men still fight.

When they do lash a prisoner, the guards are harsh and hold nothing back, so I know my target has been properly introduced to prison life. *How sad!* I think not and smile.

The guards drag both men towards the treatment table.

Hmm, it looks like my target got a few punches into the big fella too. For him, I feel bad.

"What are their names?" I ask the guards.

"This big one's Hodder, and the other poor sap is Griggs. They're new and we had to teach them respect," the guard replies, smiling proudly at his handiwork.

Taking a rag with soapy water, I gently clean Hodder's wounds. Fearful he might recognize me from being at the fence, I turn away to keep him from seeing my face. But he's so intent on watching my target on the other table that he doesn't even look my direction. Finishing, I send him back out with the guards.

Now for Griggs. This is where I'll know if he recognizes me. But maybe not, both his eyes are nearly swollen shut. Besides, I had been just a little girl, and it's been years and I've changed. But, even if he does, it doesn't matter. He lives in hell now.

The guard's eyes widen when I take a bottle of the doctor's whisky from a cupboard and pour some of it over Griggs' lashings. He screams with pain from the intense sting, but I don't care. I smile at the guards who are helping hold him down.

"He must be a sissy," I say as I rub a cloth hard across his wounds. Handing the bottle to one of the guards, I say, "Here, you keep the rest." They both grin and nod.

"He's done. Take him out," I say as I wave them away.

I know it's not over for him yet. The new prisoners have already been moved to their cells, so coming in late means you get what's left of the beds, and that's where no one wants to be — he one closest to the stench hole. Maybe he'll have to bunk with the big fella. I think not, Hodder will probably take whatever bed he wants, but Griggs will have to take the last bed, if there is one. I treasure the thought.

Later, feeling somewhat guilty, I wrestle with my feelings. This ugliness, what have I become? I mourn the innocent girl I used to be. Is she gone forever?

※※※※※

The hospital care room is extra busy today. As always, the door bangs open as guards drag another prisoner into the room. Don't they know how to enter through a door without slamming it?

This prisoner moans with pain as they carry him to one of the tables.

"This Fenian's arm is broke!" tells the guard. "A boulder in the quarry rolled loose while he was standing between the wagon and the wall of rock. Lucky for him it's only his arm."

"Should've been the bastard traitor's head," says the other, as they laugh and walk out.

I look at him thrashing around on the table and try to quiet him.

"Sarah," I tell her, "hurry. Go get the doctor."

Quickly she leaves to find him.

Trying not to add to his pain, I gently remove his shirt so Doctor Ross will be able to examine his chest and arms. It doesn't look to me that his arm is broken, but it's up to the doctor to tell.

While he's still moaning from the pain, I carefully look at his shoulder. The way it looks, I think it might be dislocated. Working here, I've learned to recognize such injuries.

As I continue to carefully inspect his body for more injuries, I run my hand over a scarred "D" branded into his chest. Taken aback at the sight, I hesitate and look at the patient only to notice him watching me.

Doctor Ross takes his time entering the room. "What's happened?"

"This man was pinned between a falling boulder and a wagon. He doesn't appear to have any other injury, just his shoulder," I say.

The doctor steps forward to examine him, then grabs his arm. I cringe because I know what's about to happen.

"Hold his feet," the doctor tells the guard, then looking at me, he says, "You hold his head."

Standing close, I hold the man ready for the quick yank on the arm. Having helped the doctor set limbs many times, I know this is going to hurt like hell. His screams wash over me as I cradle his head during the quick yank on the arm, something I never get used to hearing. Groaning with agony, he rolls his pale face towards me and looks into my eyes.

Wiping sweat from his face, I tell him, "You'll be all right now. It's over."

"Bind him up," orders Doctor Ross as he and the guard walk away.

While I wrap a clean cloth around his shoulder, I ask, "What's your name?"

"What does it matter?" he replies.

Looking at him, I shrug. "I like to know who I'm helping. It's all I have in this ugly place."

"This prison is a graveyard of living hell," he says, with sadness in his eyes.

Nodding, I agree. "I heard the guard call you one of the Fenians. I've always heard stories about your cause."

"Aye, so what of it?"

I shrug again. "Your group is somewhat of a legend around here. I heard you gave Her Majesty somewhat of a hard time back in England."

What am I doing? What is all this shrugging my shoulders?

I get brave and ask, "Why did they hot iron a 'D' on your chest?"

80

He doesn't answer, but looks away. I realize I shouldn't have asked.

Finishing wrapping his shoulder, I tell him, "If you can, try not to use your arm."

Still moaning with pain, he sits up, and I help him put his torn shirt back on. "You'll just have to manage the best you can. Be careful."

Two guards come back in, "Quit takin' so long. You've done enough." They pull him to his feet and push him out through the door.

"What's your name?" I ask him again.

He turns. Then, tipping his head while holding his arm, "Wilson. James Wilson."

I smile. *Well, Mr. Wilson, you can hurt yourself anytime.*

⁂

I have it better than most girls. Even though the doctor doesn't need me in the hospital or his bed as much these days, he makes sure to let the guards know I'm still his and they're to leave me alone. So that makes things a little safer for me. But since he's been seeing Rou, he's requesting me less and less to his bed. And before long, he isn't seeing me at all, which is a relief. Does he know I'm carrying his baby?

My blood hasn't come for several months now, and my breasts hurt as they grow larger. I don't want to tell anyone, especially the doctor. Maybe I'm hoping it will go away.

Sick most of the time, I'm unable to keep my food down. I see the girls watching me and whispering. I know they suspect something. But still, I haven't told them and try to hide it. Maybe I'm ashamed.

Being extra careful around the guards, I try to avoid them by keeping my head down and working. Soon it's unavoidable, and I see them looking at me with disgust when they notice my belly. They don't like seeing any of us girls pregnant.

It's not long before I feel my baby move inside. It's a butterfly feeling at first. Each day as I wake, I'm eager to feel it again, but then, it makes me sad. I know I won't get to keep it, and might not even get

81

to hold it, but for now, I can love my baby. The butterfly feeling soon becomes a kick as my baby grows.

"Let me feel it move," says Orla.

"Me too. I want to feel it," says Liz, as they both gather around.

We all sit on my bunk and as they put their hands on my belly, I look over at Yuliya and see the sadness on her face. Remembering the birth of her baby some years back, my heart goes out to her.

"Come on," I say to her, motioning her over. Her face lights up with a smile as she joins us.

I think my baby is happy today. It must like my friends, by the way it moves and kicks for them. For now, the four of us laugh and savor this little bit of happiness.

Seven months have gone by, and it's getting harder for me to stand all day as my baby continues to grow.

I've finished cooking meals for the pigs, so I grab the dirty pots, and make my way over to the water pump. I see Rou washing pans and sit on a stool next to her. Working together it's one of the few times we can talk freely.

Thinking back to happier times, Rou listens as I tell stories of my home back in England.

I share a memory from when I was a little girl helping my mum in the kitchen. "There was one time I washed the dishes for my mum and thought I did a good job. Later, I noticed she was washing them over again. I guess I didn't do so good."

We both laugh, then I ask Rou, "Do you remember much about your family?"

"Oh, I don't 'members no family. D'ems taken us apart when I was just wee little. I had no schooling like you. I grew up helping in a big house till the Master, him died. Then somehows dey want me here. So here I is. It wasn't bad, not like here."

16

Carrying the kettles and pots into the supply keep, I look over at the partially hidden door at the far end of the room. It's always puzzled me, so I get curious to see what's behind it and where it leads. Maybe it's a way to escape.

I point the door out to Rou. "Look, let's see what's behind it."

Hesitating and unsure, she asks, "You think we must?"

"No one will know. They won't miss us for a little while."

Going over to the dirty window, I look out and see two guards standing around talking. They probably don't know we're in here.

"It's all right; no one's watching."

I can't move the table though, it's too heavy. "Here Rou, help me push it away from the door."

Carefully we slide the table just enough so we can open the door and squeeze through. Just inside, dusty stone steps lead to the darkness below.

"This is scary," Rou says.

"Go grab some glims and a striker," I tell her. "I saw some piled on one of the tables."

Quickly, she's back with two. Lighting them, we slowly move down the first step. Hesitating, I take a deep breath. "Stay close to me."

As we go down the steps, Rou whispers, "You know, where I comes from, the dead people walk around in places like 'dis. The old witch doctor says, you must respect 'em, and leave 'em alone, or 'dey will do awful things to you. I'm tell'n you, Adeleen, I've seen 'em. We must go back. We mus'nt go down der. Please, Adeleen, I wan'a go back up now, before dem's take me." She tugs frantically on my sleeve.

"No, I want to see more." Grabbing her hand, I pull her farther down the steps into the dark. "I've heard about this place," I whisper to her. "It must be where a guard told me prisoners used to be taken, never to see daylight again. They call it the 'dark dungeon.' I wager this is it."

"I think you be right. 'Dis is it. 'Dis the dark dungeon, all right," says Rou in a shaky voice.

A small amount of light comes in through the slits in the stone walls. With the flickering flames from the glims, my eyes soon adjust as we move down to the bottom step. More curious than ever, I go further, dragging Rou behind.

"We's probably should go back now, Missy Adeleen," she begs, tugging harder on my sleeve.

We enter a large room, which smells of rats that make this place their home. I glimpse one as it scampers across the floor. I'm starting to get scared, but I don't want Rou to know. Even I begin to think we shouldn't be down here.

Looking around, I see chains hanging from iron rings bolted securely to the stone — chains that must have cruelly secured the prisoners. I can't imagine. I was in chains on the ship that brought me to Australia. But, to live my life chained to a wall, I cringe at the thought.

All of a sudden, a cold chill engulfs us, blowing out our glims. We feel the cold of death that lingers here, and Rou and I scream. She lets go of my arm and runs up the steps towards the door.

I hesitate, but really, do I want to be here alone in the dark? She's right, we shouldn't be here. Quickly, I start up the steps, but half way up I trip on my skirt and fall. Screaming, I tumble to the bottom. The rats quickly leap on my legs, biting me with their sharp teeth.

Rou screams, "Dem ghost got you, 'dey got you, Adeleen, run!"

I get up, batting them away, and hurry up the steps where Rou is waiting. Shaking, we quickly close the door and shove the table against it. As I hold my stomach, we look at each other.

Bolting in through the door, one of the guards yells, "What the hell's going on in here?"

Thinking quickly, I pick up a small pot with a handle and stand there like I'm ready to kill something.

"Nothing, sir. We just saw a giant rat," I answer.

"Well, you two just get the hell back to the kitchen, or I'll lock ya in here to spend the night with 'em," he says.

I see Rou standing frozen and wide-eyed. " Es, sir !" she nods. Turning to me she says, "We best get back."

I quickly agree. Shaking from the ordeal, I move past the guard holding the door open, and make straightway to the kitchen.

I'll never get curious enough to go back through that door leading down those steps. Like Rou tells me, "Best leave that ghost alone. It might get me." I think maybe she was right.

⬥⬥⬥⬥⬥

Back in the kitchen, I feel a sharp pain, then something warm running down my legs. Fearing the worst, I look down. Is it blood? No, it's not. Something is wrong though. It's too early for my baby to be born. Did I hurt it falling down those steps in the dungeon?

Looking around I see the guards standing in the shade leaning against the wall of a building across the way. Like most of the time, they're talking, laughing, and doing nothing.

Not wanting them to know I'm in labor, I avoid looking their way to avoid any kind of parlay with them. Carrying several pots over to the water trough I sit on a small stool and begin washing them. Taking my time scrubbing, my labor pains worsen. I know I can't stay here, I need to do something.

Getting up I take a deep breath, then slowly carry the pots to the supply room. Grabbing the handle and pushing my way inside, I quickly shut the door behind me. Tossing the pots onto the table, I look for a place to lie down. Hiding in here for a while will be good. Hopefully, no one will notice I'm missing.

I pull off a large cloth that covers the supplies, and take it to spread on the floor in the corner where I can lie down. Looking over

85

at the door that leads below and thinking it might be a safe place to hide, I remember the rats and the ghost. Even though I'm scared and don't want to be alone, I realize it's better to stay here.

Closing my eyes, I try not to fight but let the pains of labor move across my stomach. No wonder Yuliya yelled, but I can't. I have to be quiet. Pulling the cloth to my mouth, I try to muffle my screams.

The labor is painful, and becomes intense. Staring at the door to the outside and fighting with my decision to go to the hospital, I stay on the floor with my back against the wall.

It's hot in this building since all the windows are closed. Taking quick short breaths, and biting on a cloth to endure, I feel sweat dripping down my face. Unable to bear the pain any longer, I finally decide I must go.

Making my way out of the storage room, I see the sun is close to setting, and the air outside is cooler. The guards have moved on, probably to find a girl for the night. Moving past the kitchen, and holding my stomach, I brace myself with each contraction.

"Oh no, you's in labor," a welcome voice says.

I look up and see Rou as she reaches out to take my hand.

"I can help you as long as dose guards don't stop me," she says, taking my arm and putting it over her shoulder.

Smiling at her, I say, "I'm so happy to see you."

Entering the birthing room, we're met by Mary and Helen, two older women who midwife the births. I've worked at the hospital with both of them, so I feel safe with them. Helen takes me to an empty bed as I see Mary talking to Rou and shaking her head no.

Rou looks over at me and gives me a wave. Sadly, I watch my friend leave.

My labor continues for hours, and like Yuliya, I cry out. I wish Rou could have stayed with me. I so need my friend. My labor goes on well into the night, wearing me out, making me want to take a break and come back and finish all of this another time. But that's not going to happen. The pains are coming one on top of another, giving me little time to rest.

Then, I feel the baby coming. Holding Mary's hand, I push, but the baby doesn't come. Helen reassures me it's close, and to take three big breaths, and push again, and again, and then again. Finally, I hear a wee tiny cry.

Quickly turning away, I don't want to see it. I don't want to see what those bastards have done to me. But, after a moment I remember how my baby kicked inside me, and how I loved it.

Frightened that they've already taken my baby away, I quickly turn back and reach out. Helen sees me and understands that I want to see my baby. Laying the baby in my arms, she whispers, "It's a girl."

Carefully I unwrap the rag of a blanket to see my tiny baby girl. Putting my face to her soft cheek, my tears roll down onto her beautiful skin.

Holding her close, I whisper, "So you're the one who's been kicking me."

I know they'll take her soon, so I relish every second with her. She's so small; little fingers, and toes — not a full-term baby, with probably little chance of surviving. *Did I cause you to be born too early when I fell down those steps?* Closing my eyes and taking a deep breath, I inhale her sweet smell.

"I want to name you before they take you. What shall I call you? Rose. That's it, I'll call you, Rose. Even if it's just for a little while, your name will be Rose," I whisper in her wee ear. Too tiny to even suckle, she lies quiet against my breast as we both rest.

Sometime later, Mary and Helen wake me. It's time to let Rose go. I feel I might go crazy as my heart is ripped away, but even so, I don't fight. Rose can't stay in this ugly prison, so I let her go, praying she will have a better life than me. As I hand her to Mary, I kiss her wee little head and make a promise to Rose. *Not a day will go by that I won't think about you, my Rose.* I close my eyes and turn my face as they walk away.

I have to go back to my ugly life. It's hard though. I look at life differently now, with a new sadness, and purpose. I now will risk everything to find a way of escape. I wish I could go and get Rose, but where? Maybe I will find her someday.

My heart aches as I close my eyes, remembering how I held her to my breast. Then I open them, and my heart breaks all over again. So, I try to not think about her too much, but that's impossible. She's my Baby Rose. I don't even know if she's still alive, she was so tiny.

I know there are women from the community outside who came and took her. I've seen the midwives give other babies to them at the door, and watch them as they carry those babies away. They go somewhere, maybe an orphanage? My mind swirls with thoughts. Determined, I have to do something, I must find out where Rose is.

A week later I see Helen working alone. I cross the room, and head straight for her. I need to know where they took Rose. I want to somehow go and find her.

"Helen! You have to tell me where she is."

Trying to walk away from me, she shakes her head. Following right behind her, I won't stop until I have an answer.

"Helen! I'm not going to leave until you tell me where she is. Please, I beg you."

"You don't want to know," she tells me. "It will only cause you more pain."

"What?"

Looking at me with a sad stoic face, she tells me, "She didn't live. Your baby was too small and didn't survive. When we took her from your arms, she was already dead."

"Don't tell me that. Why are you saying that? No! Rose is alive, and you took her, I remember."

"No child, I'm sorry, it's true. That's why you never heard her cry but that once after she was born."

I scream, "I don't believe you! You're lying! You took her, I saw you! I know you're lying!"

"No, Adeleen, I'm sorry."

As Helen reaches out to comfort me, I push her away. "You're evil! You stole my baby." Rage welling up within me, I shriek, "I'll kill you!" as I grab her. Helen screams for the guards and tries to pull away from my grip. Two guards hear the ruckus, and come running into the room. Grabbing me, they pull me from her. With a gut wrenching cry, I let go as the guards drag me away to be lashed.

It takes months before I set foot in the birthing room again. Over time, I make amends to Helen. She knows I'm hurting and understands. Now, every time I see a pregnant woman my heart hurts for her. I know the hell she will suffer.

17

Going to the guards' quarters to drop off their laundry, I see keys hanging on a hook. As I reach to take them, a hand comes from behind and stops me.

"Now what do you think you're doing?" asks Palmer.

"Nothing. I saw the keys on the floor and picked them up to put them back."

"Oh, were you now? I thought they were already hanging there."

"No sir, I tell you, I picked them up."

"You're lying," he says, as he grabs my blouse and pulls my face right up to his.

"No, sir," I tell him again, "I picked them up."

Slapping me across the face, he shoves me. "Get out a' here."

With my head down to avoid any more abuse, I quickly go out the door. Feeling something run from my nose, I pull up my blouse and wipe. The damn ratbag's given me a nose bleed.

***

I've gotten to know most of the guards who work here. Remembering some of their faces from times past. The rapes, beatings, and their just plain meanness. But there's one guard, Hadley, who I particularly remember. He's the one who kicked Emma, killing her. Every time I see him, I remember my promise to her — I will get even.

The fat slob comes into the eating room every day, acting like he's the best guard around. His smug attitude is even disliked by most of the other guards. They know he's mean. I spit or put something filthy in his meal whenever I can get away with it.

Although one day as I spit, Lieutenant Samuel walks in, looking straight at me. At first I freeze, and then I nod towards the repulsive guard. The Lieutenant looks, then cocks his head as to say, "Give it to him." How's that for loyalty among the guards?

After that, the lieutenant and I had something unspoken between us. He doesn't seem to be as heartless as some of the other guards. I think he might have to appear mean, or none of the prisoners would respect him. But, I still, don't like him.

The doctor isn't calling me to his bed anymore. Maybe it's because of the baby, I don't know and don't care. Besides, he's found other girls who meet his needs, and that's fine with me. I'm glad to get away from him, although I miss the baths.

There isn't a moment I don't think about Rose. Did Mary and Helen tell him about her? Did he ever go to see her? I've never asked them, and I'm not sure I want to know. But, I try not to think of it too much, or else I'll drive myself crazy. I have to let her go.

It's not long before Lieutenant Samuel hears that I'm no longer seeing the doctor and takes me as his. When he calls for me, he very seldom sends me back to my cell. He doesn't make my life easy, which reminds me I'm still in prison. I always knew he liked me. So, once again I'm safe from being passed around. The guards soon get the message, don't touch. I've even heard Lieutenant Samuel tell them, "Hands off!"

He's a handsome man. Black hair, mustache, and those white britches and his uniform make me swoon. Liz thinks I'm the lucky one for catching his eye, but it's never lucky to be used by any man.

The military officers always go home to England after, maybe, five years. Over the years, I've gotten to know some of the officers in their dashing red coats. But, this is the first time one of them has taken me for his own.

Lieutenant Samuel has been here for about a year, so he'll probably not have to leave for a few more years. That's good for me…that is, if he decides to keep me. I live with that fear though, and I'm always afraid, so I treat him well, and pray he'll keep me.

Most of the non-military guards can go back to England after ten years of service, if they want. But, then there are those guards who can never go back because England doesn't even want them. They are told they have to stay. These are the ones who are the meanest, and we know who they are. Everyone needs to watch out around them because they're dangerous.

Over time I get to know Lieutenant Samuel, and he shares with me what some of the newer guards are like. He doesn't know that I need this information if I ever want to escape. So, I learn to know what guards to avoid, who are lazy and who are weak. The lieutenant avoids trying to get too close emotionally with me, but he needs someone to help him to survive this hell, and for now, it's me.

I learn to take care of him and not fight him like I did the others. I treat him better than most, and that makes a big difference in how he treats me. I not only fulfill his needs in bed, but I also care for him in many other ways. I'll pick up after him, and hang up his uniform that is left on the chair. I so want him to keep me and not throw me away.

At night, when we're together, he talks about the prison, probably more than he should. But he's built up a trust in me, and that makes me feels safe. Maybe he needs me. I listen and find useful things he shares with me, like who the guards at the prison are who like men instead of women. Now, that's information I can use.

One evening while walking back to the lieutenant's quarters, I see the two guards, the ones Lieutenant Samuel told me who like men. Boldly walking up to them, I tell them, "I hear the new prisoner Griggs likes men. He wants a visit from you, if you know what I mean."

They look at each other and smile, then quickly head towards the cellblock. As I walk on, I hear the guards ask for Griggs by name. I stop and watch from behind a post, as Griggs comes forward to be let out of his cell, and then he's told to follow them.

As I go back to the lieutenant's room, I think about how much I miss my Rose, Mum, and Benjamin.

18

The local natives bring a body into the yard today. It's Asa. He came up missing two weeks ago. He never came back from working at the quarry. The guards didn't seem to worry. They knew it would only be a matter of time until his body was found, providing he tried to escape across the desert and not the sea. If he tried to swim the sea, then the sharks would have him, and most likely nothing would be left.

But Asa chose to try the desert. His body's a gruesome sight. The sun has baked him dry. His eyes are gone, maybe from the birds, or bugs. His tongue has swollen out of his mouth three times larger than it should be. His body is blistered and burnt. It appears he had taken off his shirt, but the sun made quick on his skin. He's lucky the wild dogs didn't find him. They would have torn him apart.

The guards leave Asa's body in the yard for several days for all to see as a reminder, there's no escaping from the Establishment.

I cry. My hope of ever finding a way out of this place seems more impossible than ever, but still, I won't give up hope.

Daily, I work in a more lax part of the prison. Thanks to Lieutenant Samuel, I've been given more freedom. Behaving myself helps. I'm now able to walk down to the pier for fresh fish and order market supplies. Some of the guards don't like me going out the gate. They probably think I won't come back. But still, I have nowhere to go if I should try, so I always return.

The hair on the back of my neck stands up as I see Griggs carrying produce into the kitchen with Mychael and Louie.

"Adeleen," says, Mychael, "where do you want these put?"

"Over there," I say pointing to space next to the chest

I feel Griggs's piercing eyes taking a long look at me as he tries to remember me. I fear it won't take him long before he does. Staying busy, I shudder from what I know could be coming.

"Adeleen…hey, I remember that name," says Griggs. "You're that little red-haired rat who killed her father."

Mychael looks over at me. "Everything all right, Miss Adeleen?"

"Yes," I answer.

Mychael steps outside but stands by the door with Louie, listening and waiting for Griggs. They know my story, so it's not a shock to them. I've told Mychael everything about why I'm in prison.

Not saying a word, I stare back at Griggs.

"Aye, you're that little brat. We sent you and your brother to the Australian prisons to be rid of you."

Benjamin? My heart races at hearing his name and learning he might be here too. *When was he sent here?*

Not wanting to extend the conversation with Griggs too much, I don't ask. *But then…my mum, what of her?*

"What happened to my mum?" I ask.

"Oh her, she's not much better off than you. Last I heard, his family ran her out of town, and now she's a gutter whore."

Griggs walks towards me. I look at one of the guards who's within shouting distance. But, instead, I reach over and grab one of the cutting knives. Holding it in front of me, I'm not afraid to use it. It's bigger than my rusty knife, and I'd take joy in ripping him apart.

"That's close enough," I tell him. My eyes widen with hate as I listen to his words spewing out of his mouth.

"That's right. I remember when we sent your sorry little arse away."

Yes, but he doesn't remember the hospital care room. I think his face was too smashed to be able to see.

"You're right. I'm that little girl, all grown up." Standing in defiance, I say, "You'd better caution yourself. I know more killers besides myself here, and any one of them will be happy to do anything I ask."

Staring back at me for a moment, he nods.

"Good, we have an understanding," I say.

"Which is…?" he asks.

"Watch yourself and stay away from me, and live," I tell him.

Hearing that, he goes outside to where Mychael and Louie are waiting.

Watching them walk away, tears run down my cheeks as I think of my mum and Benjamin. My heart aches.

Benjamin! If he's here, I must find him.

❦❦❦❦❦

Hearing a commotion outside, I look out the window of the kitchen into the yard and see cattle coming down the dirt road. Someone has turned them loose to stampede into the prison. They're running at full speed, frightened, and unaware of where they're going. There's a loud crashing noise as three steers enter through the doorway into the eating room, horns down, and ready to smash anything or anyone who gets in their way.

One plows into the kitchen where we're preparing the meal. Screaming, Liz, Rou, and I jump up onto anything we can to get out of the way of the angry beast. I hear the guards yelling, trying to herd the cattle out.

Standing on a table, Liz yells at me, "What'll I do?"

"Hell, I don't know. Just stay where you are — up out of its way."

I safely perch myself in the window sill of the stone wall. Liz screams, and jumps off the table. Gasping, I scream as I watch her try to get over to where I am. The bull turns to hook her with his large horns but slips on the mashed food it smeared all over the floor. Just as the bull regains his footing, he charges at her again.

Reaching down with both hands, I grab her arms and pull her up before she's hurt.

Out of breath, we sit watching the bull continue to thrash around in the kitchen, jamming at the pots, catching one on its horns and ramming into everything as it skids on the floor. It's getting harder for its hoofs to find traction and the beast keeps slipping and falling. The poor thing is scared out of its wits just like us.

95

The cabinet Rou is on topples as the bull rams it, falling over on top of the animal. Rou screams and jumps off, racing to the corner of the kitchen, and hides behind a big barrel full of flour.

"Watch out, Rou!" I scream as I see the bull plow towards her.

The barrel breaks apart and flour flies everywhere. Rou tries to protect herself, huddling behind another barrel as the bull goes to tear it apart too.

She stays huddled as it's rammed by the raging bull. Screaming, she finally runs and finds another safe place.

Finally, one of the guards comes in, waving his arms and yelling, trying to turn the animal back through the door. Slipping and sliding, the animal drops its head, trying to hook him, but misses. It is soon headed back through the kitchen door and runs down the road with one of our pots hooked on its horn. Then it's quiet.

We stay in our safe places and look at our demolished kitchen. Everything is smashed. Soup is spilled on the floor and splattered on the walls. Potatoes are mashed and all over the room. The meat is on the floor, along with flour everywhere — what a mess.

Looking at Rou, both Liz and I start laughing.

Her face and clothes are covered with white flour, and it's hard even to recognize her.

"Why, Rou, you look like a ghost," I say.

The three of us stand there looking at all the mess, and then we start laughing again.

"Well, there goes their dinner," I say, as I reach down to the floor with a large fork and skew the large piece of meat that's been cooking on the stove. "The guards can still eat this," plopping it in a pot.

Our laughter becomes uncontrollable as we enjoy seeing the mess. Even though we will be the ones to clean it all up, it's worth it. Besides, the guards aren't going to be eating for a while.

"Too bad this doesn't happen every day," says Liz. "The guards might have to eat off the floor."

"Dat's funny," says Rou. "Maybe dey should let dem dere cows out more often, den dey wouldn't be so nasty and mean."

One of our best days!

19

Working on cleaning up the mess the bull made, I see Mychael bringing supplies. He comes inside to look at the destroyed kitchen.

"What happened?" he asks.

"Oh, not much, we just had an unwelcomed visitor called a bull," I say.

Walking closer to me, he whispers telling me there's a group of Irish rebel prisoners, called the Fenians, are planning an escape.

I look at Mychael, slowly nodding that I'm interested.

How did he find out? How many people know about this? Mychael is trustworthy, so I don't think he would share this information with just anyone.

Thinking back, I remember the Fenian I helped care for in the hospital. There have been many escape plots planned; most never happen, or some try only to end up dead. But for some reason, this one interests me, maybe because, like me, they're Irish.

A few days later, I see two Fenians while on my way to market to get some fish. One of them is James Wilson, the one I remember from the hospital. They're returning from working at the limestone hills where the stone quarry is.

It's risky, but I approach them. I quickly look around to make sure no guard is watching, and stop to tell them I know what they're planning and I can help.

The looks on their faces grow dark. Well, they will either kill me or let me be a part of their escape. I tell them I can get valuable information and supplies for them. I'm lying, but they don't know.

They look at each other, and then one says they will get back to me. Until then I'm to keep my mouth shut. If I breathe a word of it to anyone, I will find myself dead.

I hurry off with my heart racing with hope.

Going back to the kitchen, I realize just how dangerous this could be. It could mean our lives if we get caught. I shiver at the thought. Taking a deep breath I get brave. I know it will take all my courage, but I'm ready to take the risk with them. I feel the excitement growing within me as I pray they will believe what I told them.

Curious what their plan is, I wonder, will we be able to pull this off? Well, if they're willing then so am I, even if I die trying.

Through the years, I have seen and heard many stories of those who attempted to escape. But all resulted in death. Like Asa. He died in the desert, and the guards left his body to rot in the yard for all of us to see.

But I'm ready to take the risk. I finally have my chance to get away from this wretched place, and have the will within me to be brave. So, I cling to the hope of escape and pray they will let me go with them.

The days are sweltering as the summer is ending, and anyone making a break in this heat probably won't survive. But since the rain will soon be upon us, maybe the escape will work.

What's taking so long? Are they going to let me in on their plan or not? Yes, I'm impatient, but still I wait.

Working in the kitchen today, I'm able to watch at the window as prisoners walk back from their jobs. Very seldom am I needed at the hospital, and that's all right with me. I have more freedom working in the kitchen. At times I take the rubbish to the dump outside the prison walls, or I'm given the task to go down to the harbor to buy fresh fish for the meals. This is one of my favorite freedoms. I enjoy the chance to walk outside and get away from the prison.

As I walk from the kitchen to toss scraps into the chicken pen, I notice one of the Fenians motioning to me. I give a quick eye motion in the direction of a guard who is watching me. The Fenian blinks that he understands, and keeps walking. What did he want to tell me, are they going to let me help? The answer will just have to wait, but what? My mind races with excitement.

I'm timing my going outside every day to when the prisoners come back from work. I make it easy for the men to see me but try to look busy so the guards won't suspect anything.

With my basket I walk in the direction of James and others coming back in. Suddenly I drop what I'm carrying, and he quickly stops to help.

"I have to meet with you," he whispers as he helps me pick up the contents. "It will be dangerous, so we have to be very careful."

The guard yells, "Get along!"

I quickly nod to the guard.

"Meet me by the gate," James whispers as he walks away.

Not wanting the guard to notice, I linger with my basket but soon follow some distance behind.

Walking past the stone roundhouse and over to the large gate, James turns into a narrow space between the building and the stone walls, and a few minutes later I follow.

Stopping by a large rock then looking to see if anybody's watching, he bends down and lifts the bush to one side, revealing a large board. He lifts it, and I see an opening that goes underground.

"Get in," he urges, nudging me to hurry and drop down into the dark. I put my basket behind the bush then hesitate, thinking back to the ghost in the dungeon that scared the hell out of me. I'm not too keen on going down into a dark hole.

He gives me a rather hearty push, and I fall in, with him dropping right behind me. Quickly he reaches up to cover the opening.

It's dark and takes a moment for my eyes to adjust. Seeing a dim flickering light at the end of the short tunnel, I get down on my knees and begin to crawl. Pushing on my behind, he encourages me to hurry up. I want to turn around and slap him and yell, *Get your hands off my bum!* But I don't.

Moving forward, I'm able to stand upright and walk a few steps forward into a torch-lit room. Brushing the dirt off my dress, I frown and look back at James, but he just smiles. He knows I want to slug him. Looking around, I again remember the room with the ghost and take a deep breath trying to shake off the creepy feeling.

Knowing we're somewhere under the prison in a storage room that's probably been forgotten long ago, after the prison was first built. How did they find this place?

Standing in front of me are four men. Mychael told me how these men were sent to Fremantle Prison because of their political fight against the British government. So, these are some of the Fenian troublemakers, I think as I look at them — members of the Irish Republican Brotherhood, a real thorn in England's side. I can't believe I'm standing here with them.

As they look at me in silence trying to size me up, I feel uncomfortable. What are they thinking? Finally, James Wilson begins to speak, asking me questions, and then one by one the men start asking too.

"We want to know what connections you have here at the prison, and why do you think you can help us?" says one of them.

"Where, and what information can you get us about the vessels in the harbor?" asks another.

I tell them that I work in the kitchen and the hospital. I often overhear the guards when they know about any upcoming escape attempts, and what they plan to do about it. That should perk their ears.

I also mention that I know where the guards keep their guns, and that I could get access to the keys to unlock the armory.

I know the schedules the guards' work, which guards to be careful around, and which ones are lazy. I also mention that I go to the port almost daily and can find out when ships are coming and going in the harbor and how long they will be in port.

Standing to one side, they put their heads together. I hear them argue. "We need her," says James. "She has access to the ships coming into the harbor."

They look at me. "I don't care," one says. "What if she should say something?"

"She won't. Look, I see her go to the port every day to get food. I know she's telling the truth. They won't suspect a thing. Something

100

must have happened to the ship, and she might be able to find out for us," says James.

"You may be right, but she'd better keep her trap shut," says one of the men, raising his voice loud enough for me to hear.

They look at each other, and one of them tells me they will get back to me. Until then I'm to keep my mouth shut. If I breathe a word of it to anyone, I will find myself dead…drawing his finger across his throat.

James takes me back to the tunnel, and together we crawl up out of the hole. Not waiting around, I grab my basket and hurry off as my heart races with excitement.

I knew they would find me valuable, although a lot of what I told them isn't quite true. But still, maybe they realize if they're to succeed, they will need my help.

❦❦❦❦❦

Days go by, and I don't hear anything. Then finally, one day while passing James, he walks close enough to slips me a scrap of paper. Quickly, I tuck it into the waistband of my skirt. I'll have to look at it later when I'm alone. Feeling unsettled, I worry. They don't know I can't read.

Alone in the lieutenant's room, I stare at the note while keeping it hidden in case he should come in. What does it say? I look at all the scribbles, unable to remember what I learned long ago as a child. I remember some of the letters, but don't know how to put them into words. I should have paid more attention in school instead of looking out the window so much.

What should I do? I can't let anyone read it or tell them about my escape plans, so I do nothing. I worry, while trying to understand what it says.

The next day I see James, and I make a small head movement that means "no." I don't know what he'll think it means, but maybe he'll try to get with me again and tell me what's happening. I don't want any notes.

I pay more attention to what the men are doing, and notice some of the Fenians work on the labor crews who are sent out from the prison very early in the morning, and don't come back until just before sunset. From the kitchen window, I watch what's happening in the yard. Before long, I spot James walking back from the quarry.

Quickly, I grab a bucket to get water from the pump. When I pass him, I slow and whisper that I can meet at the side of the building at dusk, while the guards are eating their meal.

"Watch for me to come outside the kitchen," I whisper.

He gives a slight nod and quickly walks on.

The guards are filling their faces and drinking, so when their bellies are full, I'll sneak out. A bit later, most are still sitting in the eating room drinking their ale, so they won't notice what I do.

Between the buildings, James finds me waiting. He is such a good-looking man. I remember back to the first time we met in the hospital care room. He moves close to me so we can talk without being heard. He's so close that I feel his breath on my cheek. It's then I realize I have never before been as close to a man I don't hate. A tingling feeling of warmth floods my body.

"We need your help," he whispers into my ear.

Not wanting him to see what effect he has on me, I whisper back. "How?"

"We're looking for a certain ship to arrive in the harbor." Then he passes me another note. "This is the name of the ship. Let one of us know if it's in the harbor, or when it arrives."

I open the note and see one word, '*Catalpa.*'

Well, that should be easy. I think to myself. I can always match the letters.

I look at him and whisper, "I will."

Suddenly we hear someone coming. Quickly James leans against me, pinning me to the wall as we remain still. Standing there for what seems like the longest time, I feel the warmth of his body. Even after the danger passes, he continues to hold me against the wall. Then slowly he backs up and whispers "I'll be in touch with you in two days," and he's gone.

What just happened?

It's been months since James gave me the note with the name of the ship. Every other day I go with Wally, one of the younger guards, to the crowded, dock to get fresh vegetables and fish for the officers' and guards' meals.

I pass by a list of the ships posted on a board. I don't know what the board says about the ships, but I still look for the word. I can't read, but I can match the letters, I'm sure of it. I've memorized them all, so if any of the names look like it, I will check my note to make sure.

One does look like it might be, so I take out my paper to compare, forgetting Wally is close. Passing by the big ship, I peer at the name painted on its hull. No, it doesn't match. Where is the ship? It's been so long, but I won't give up looking.

"What you got there? What you looking at, missy?" asks Wally.

Shrugging my shoulders, making a curious face, I say, "Don't know, nothing in particular." He reaches out, so I have to hand the paper to him. It's all tattered and worn from me taking it in and out of my pocket and looks to be something someone has thrown away.

"Ah, it ain't nothing," he says, tossing it to the ground.

When he turns his back, I drop the fish I'm carrying and scurry to pick it and the wadded paper up, hiding it in the big fish's mouth. Wally looks back, but I've already hidden it. *He's stupid,* I think as I look and smile at him. I'm glad I already bought the fish, but now my note's going to be slimy.

Together we get the supplies, and he helps me pull the wagon back up the hill to the prison. It always takes some time, so we never hurry. I use it to think about what I will do after I escape. Not knowing anything other than this prison, my thoughts don't go far. What will it be like to be free?

As we walk through the large iron gates and past the stone roundhouse inside the prison, I'm sorry that I have to give the Fenians the sad news again. As Wally and I walk towards the kitchen, we pass Thomas. I slightly shake my head "no." Disappointment shows on his face as he walks past us.

Week, after week, I have to give the same news. Will their ship ever get here? I see their empty faces every time I come back with a "no." I'm starting to worry their ship might be lost at sea.

Yet, the men don't give up hope, so neither should I. But it's hard. Hanging onto their hope with them, I keep thinking, maybe in a few days, just maybe. I know it will come.

It has to, I can feel it.

20

Walking towards the dock today, I hear a ship's bell announcing its entry into the harbor. I struggle to know if it's the ship, I can only see the mast, but attached to the very top is a thin green ribbon streaming in the wind.

I tell Wally, let's run, I want to see the ship come into the harbor. He's young and agrees, so we start running.

My heart beats with hope, it must be it. It has to be the ship. I continue to hear her bell ringing, as the ship drops her sails, slowly drifting into port. An Irish green ribbon must be a signal. It must be.

Not wanting to bring attention to how excited I am, I slow to skip and start to sing, so Wally only suspects I'm in a good mood today.

By the time we get to the harbor, the ship is already docked and is being moored to the pier. I look at the letters painted on her hull and see the same word that was written on the paper given to me many months ago. Letters so etched into my memory that I no longer need my note: *Catalpa.*

There she is, tall and beautiful with her sails folded from the wind. She's holding a secret that I know. It's a whaling ship, and she's finally here. Looking up at her tall masts, I think her voyage across the sea must have been difficult because she's so late. But she's finally here, and our hope has arrived!

The Royal Navy officers come running. Wally walks over to see what the commotion is all about, and I'm right behind him listening as the officers quickly board the *Catalpa* asking the Captain why they dropped anchor in this harbor. I hear the sailors from the ship telling the dock workers the chronometer had broken, and is in need of repairs.

It must have been a hard journey; no wonder she's so late.

I tell Wally, "We're taking too long, we need to get back with the food." Nodding, he helps me gather the fish and other supplies, then scurry off to the prison. I keep telling him, "We're late. Hurry."

Losing no time, we enter the prison through the iron gates. I see Thomas Darragh standing with a group of men who's come back from working at the quarry.

Smiling I give a nod. Thomas's eyes widen with disbelief, so I give him a second nod, and then he walks away.

Tears fill my eyes, for I have given them the hope and good news they've been awaiting so long.

Walking slowly, I watch Thomas approach James and whisper in his ear. He quickly looks in my direction. I smile as our eyes lock, then I nod.

I turn and walk away for fear of getting caught, but my heart is bursting with joy. Our escape will really happen! I know how risky it will be, but I don't care anymore. I want to leave this hell or die.

Over the next few days, the Fenians pass me several more notes — this time to deliver. My help is certainly needed, and I sense they're grateful just from the smiles they give me.

Robert Cranston nods his head to get my attention as he walks towards me. We've worked out a system: a slight nod means for me to pay attention or a tipped head to the side means to meet in the passageway. He passes me another damn note, then whispers, "As you pass by the church on your way to the port, give this to Thomas. He's working there today."

Panicking, I whisper, "Which Thomas?"

"The tall one, Hassett!"

"Two Thomas's, I get them mixed up," I grumble as I walk away. Why can't one be called Frank, or Miles? Why two Thomas's?

Getting the cart ready to take down to the market, Guard Tenley tells me Wally's busy and to go on ahead. There's a guard waiting at the pier. Perfect! I'll be able to deliver the note.

"I'll need two helpers today. I have lots to get," I tell Tenley.

He grabs Simon, an older lad, and tells him to go and help. I look over the girls. Now, which one won't ask a lot of questions if I do something out of the ordinary today? Annabel. She and Simon are both young, so I know they'll be busy talking to each other. Hopefully they won't notice what I do. Waving to Tenley, we start for the pier.

When we approach the church, Thomas is nowhere outside. What should I do?

"You two go on ahead," I tell them. "But walk slow, I have something to drop off to the priest."

Arriving at the front door of the church, I take a deep breath and reach for the handle, hoping no one is watching. I push the heavy door open and quickly walk inside.

Entering a large room, I'm in awe at how angelic it is. Losing myself, I gaze at the beautiful colorful windows and the golden altar. That's probably where God sits. I haven't been inside a church since I was a small child, so I stand looking, not thinking about why I'm here.

As I gaze around, a voice startles me.

"May I help you?"

It's Father Patrick. I've seen him many times when he comes to the prison.

"Umm, yes. I'm told by one of the guards to give Thomas Hassett a message."

"I can give it to him."

"No, your Majesty, I'm told to give it to him personally."

Chuckling, he nods and says, "Just a minute, I'll fetch him."

Oh no! I'm going straight to Hell for sure. I just told a lie to one of God's important men. Straight to Hell I'm going. I know it.

Thomas comes into the sanctuary from working in another room. Frowning, I speak loudly so Father Patrick can hear.

"Captain Leon needs you to go help Sergeant Dempsey when you're finished here," I say to Thomas as I slip him the note. Then quickly, I race back out the door and down the hill to catch up with Simon and Annabel.

Stiff up! That's what I need to do — stiffen up, I tell myself, worrying about not telling the truth. Maybe God will forgive me for lying because I'm doing something helpful. Maybe He won't mind, I hope.

⁂

Three days later while I am passing James, he tips his head, a sign for me to meet him in the usual spot between the wall and the building. Walking slowly some distance behind him so as not to appear as if we're walking together, I look around to see if anyone is watching me, then quickly dart into the opening. James motions for me to move in further to where he's waiting.

He whispers. "Just a few more days and we go."

Chills of excitement run down my spine. This time he asks me to retrieve a note from a man on the dock. *That shouldn't be too hard,* I think.

"Now, Adeleen, this is probably the most important thing you're going to do for us, so listen carefully. Tomorrow, when you go to the pier to get the fresh fish, a well-dressed gentleman will approach you. He will ask, 'Are the fish good today?' You must reply, 'Can't get any fresher.' That will be a signal for him to slip you a note. Don't let anyone see you."

"But, James, how do I know he's the right man?" I whisper.

"You'll just have to trust that he is. Then the next day, when you go back to the pier, he will approach you again, and you are to slip him a note from us."

"I will." I look deep into his blue-green eyes.

Without warning, he grabs both my arms and quickly pulls me to him, kissing me. Feeling that same tingling sensation travel through my entire body, I stand spellbound.

Then he whispers in my ear, "It's almost over, Adeleen, so be very careful. These will be the last notes. Now go!" He pushes me to leave, smiling at me as I reluctantly walk away.

Stepping back out into the bright sunlight, I feel my cheeks all aflush.

"Hey! What yer doin' coming out from back there?"

A guard walks over to look between the building and the wall. Trying to distract his attention from the building, I quickly draw my skirt up to adjust my dress. Glaring at my legs, he forgets about the passageway.

"You caught me," I say. "A girl can't take a pee without you watching every minute."

"So you go to squat, hey?"

"No, sir, I don't squat, I pull up my dress and spread my legs." Then I slowly saunter away with him following close behind.

"What say you and me go back in there? I'd like to see yer legs."

Smiling at the guard, I lead him away so James can dart from the building into a group of prisoners returning from work. The group heckles me and the guard as they pass us. James makes eye contact with me and gives a quick wink.

"How about it?" the guard asks me again.

"Oh, go find yourself another wench. I have a lieutenant waiting for me." *Worthless guard!*

21

I have trouble sleeping. My stomach's all in knots from worry. Lieutenant Samuel doesn't notice and falls into a deep sleep. In my mind, I go over and over what James told me to say to the well-dressed man at the pier. I have to make sure I don't forget anything. I must get it right. Another reason I can't fall asleep is I keep thinking about that kiss.

Before long I see morning sunlight arriving.

Heading to the kitchen I find others getting ready to start their day. I do my usual routine, then make plans to head to the harbor.

"You need to hurry back from the pier. You've been taking too much time lately," hollers one of the guards.

I smile back at him. "What's the matter? You think we'll jump onto one of those big ships and sail far away from you."

"Just you hurry on up with yourself," he growls back.

Walking down to the pier with Simon and Annabel, I see the ship *Catalpa* isn't there. My heart beats faster with worry. Why isn't it tied at the dock anymore? Where has it gone?

Panic sets inside me as I walk around on the pier. Then I spot him. He's just as James told me. A tall, finely dressed, bearded man approaches, stopping at the fish table.

Composing myself, I linger, pretending to be looking over the fish before making my purchase. I tell Annabel to go over and pick out some fresh crabs on the tables farther away, knowing that Simon will follow her. I don't want them anywhere around.

Slowly the bearded man walks along the table close to where I'm standing and asks, "Are the fish good today?"

I look at him and say, "They sure are, and they can't get any fresher."

He hesitates for a moment, as if he isn't sure. After looking me over, he slips me the note. I quickly grab a large fish and put it in the cart.

I call to Annabel and Simon to help me load everything up, and we start back to the prison.

Now tomorrow I will give him the last note, and then we're ready.

❧❦❧❦❧❦

Going into the hospital late, I realize nobody knows where I've been, or what I've been doing. They don't wonder anymore, thinking I'm probably with the lieutenant.

Pointing to where the guards are waiting, Sarah tells me they've brought in an unconscious man with red hair like mine. All my friends know I've been looking for my brother. I quickly cross the room and ask what's wrong with the prisoner, but all I really want to do is see if it might be Benjamin.

"What's his name?" I ask the guards.

"Hell if I know. All I hear is them call him Coop. Why?"

I shrug and sadly shake my head.

Looking with pity at the injured man, I see his face all bloody and swollen from being beaten, along with a large gash in the back of his head.

"What happened?"

"He got a bit cocky and didn't want to take orders. So we busted his head with a club.

I look at the poor man and say to myself, *It's not Benjamin.*

I motion for the guards to take him into the room where the doctor can sew up the back of his head.

I think I've seen every redheaded male who's here at Freemantle. Benjamin must be at another prison in Australia. Maybe I've been

111

wasting my time. He might even have had a short sentence and been released already.

There's a loud commotion as four guards slam through the hospital door carrying in an unconscious guard.

One starts yelling, "Get the doc, quick!"

More guards pile in through the door, and soon the room is full of them.

It's Hadley, unconscious with his eyes rolled back in his head and blood gushing from his throat.

"What happened to him?" I ask, as if I didn't know.

"We found him this way. No one knows anything. Where's the doctor?" he yells in desperation.

"Someone, come and help me," a guard yells, holding pressure on the wound.

Standing back, the girls take their time answering this emergency. There aren't any around who like or respect any of these guards, especially this one. But today, what the guards see frightens them. Who did this, and will they be next? *What a great day!*

So there he lies struggling to breathe, the poor bastard. Only time will tell if he'll even be able to speak again. I wager not.

Coming into the room, the senior guard, Durham, questions, "What happened here?"

"Don't know. We found him slumped over where he always sits," answers one of the guards.

"Good riddance to him," yells one of the prisoners in the treatment room.

"Yea, he can go to hell," yells another.

"Here, Adeleen." The guard grabs my hand, making me put pressure on Hadley's throat. "Hold this while we lift him on the table."

Putting very little pressure on the wound, I wish the bastard would bleed to death.

"Quick, someone, fetch the doctor," Durham pleads.

"I will." Letting go of the cloth I run into the hospital where I know the doctor won't be.

"Wait," yells the guard, but it's too late. I'm gone.

Sometime later, I return to the room where the doctor and Sarah are now attending Hadley on the table. She looks at me, then looks back, continuing to help the doctor.

"Oh, there you are," I say. "I've been looking for you, Doctor.

"Never mind that — help Sarah," he snaps.

Deliberately bumping Sarah's hip, I cause her to lose her grip.

"Sorry," I say, looking at her. "Good heavens, what happened to him?"

"Someone stabbed his windpipe and vocal cords with something sharp and rusty," says Sarah as she holds instruments for the doctor "We've stopped the bleeding, but the doctor needs to close the gash."

"I guess he won't be eating for a while," I smartly remark and snicker. Both the doctor and Sarah look at me, then continue to repair the wound.

It looks like the bastard's going to live, I think, as I look down at his unconscious fat body. That's fine. At least no one will have to listen to any of his obnoxious stories any more.

"Adeleen, do you know who did this?" whispers Sarah as she searches my eyes for an answer.

"Nope, don't have a clue, and don't care," I say. "But it does look like he got his for killing Emma."

Looking at me, Sarah smiles.

"I need to go, it's my turn to work in the kitchen," I tell her as I race out.

22

The next day, I focus on planning my last revenge, which will be the hardest. I remember back to the first time I was raped, then raped again and again by the guard whose face is the first one I burned into my memory. Guard Palmer. He's still here at Fremantle Prison and is always the first in line to rape the young girls brought from the ship. After all these years, he's still destroying lives.

I have a special goodbye planned for him. I will have to get him alone and somehow render him unconscious. There's not much love lost between the guards. In fact, Palmer is hated by others so much that I'm sure I can find a guard who will help me.

Finally, it's my last day at the hospital, and I arrive late again. While sweeping the floors in the hospital, I hear the door open as they bring Palmer in. This time the doctor is already in the room. Too bad, I won't be able to waste time looking for him. The doctor yells for help.

"Come on, Adeleen," says Rachel.

"No, get Sarah to help you. I'm busy," I say, looking uninterested.

Sometime later, Rachel finds me. "You should have seen it," she says.

"What?" I ask."

"Someone castrated him and cut off his man wanker. The doctor says it looks like it was cut off by something rusty, which isn't good for him. Go and see. He's still lying there."

"No, I don't need to see." I walk towards the door. "It's time for me to go to the kitchen. I have to make a very special soup for the guards tonight."

My day is over, and I'm finally finished in the kitchen. I take extra time and stop to look at each of my friends. No one knows I'm leaving. I can't tell them goodbye, so I merely smile and wave as I walk out the door.

To the prison, I think, *Good riddance, you'll never hurt me again.* Then I walk away to spend my last night with Lieutenant Samuel.

Early in the morning, just as the sun is rising, I sneak out of the lieutenant's room and over to the apple orchard on the west side of the prison. Running through the grove, I find James waiting for me. The prison is busy with the morning workgroups, so the commotion from it all is our cover.

"The ship is gone," I tell him. "When I went to the pier yesterday, it was gone. I couldn't find you to tell you."

"Don't worry. The ship is anchored some miles out to sea," James tells me.

Where did it go when it left the harbor? "I was scared, thinking it had left without us."

"No, it's waiting out of sight," he reassures me.

Standing beside James I listen to the six men arguing. They don't want me to go, the other five Fenians; Michael Harrington, Robert Cranston, Thomas Darragh, Thomas Hassett, and Martin Hogan. But James stands his ground, and they soon give way.

An impatient voice growls, "We're losing time. Take her!"

They look deep into my eyes. I know they're probably wondering if I could be a reason they might fail. The glares say it all.

I hear their grumbling, but to no avail. James makes it clear that he's taking me.

I must stay out of their way and not anger them. I know the trip will be long and dangerous, but I'm not going to ask them for anything. I will take care of myself and pull my weight. *Just please let me go*, my heart cries.

Together we run through another small grove of trees and soon arrive at the rendezvous spot where two buggies wait. I'm surprised to see the bearded man from the harbor standing by one of the buggies, motioning for us to hurry. He looks puzzled when he sees me, but doesn't say anything.

James smiles at me as he takes my hand to help me quickly climb up. "We're going to make it, Adeleen," he says.

Stepping into the buggy, I hold tight to his arm and sit close beside him.

For miles, the horses race down a rough road until we arrive at an open beach. Turning the buggy onto the sand, I feel the horses struggle to pull their heavy load of passengers, leaving hoof prints and wheel tracks deeply imbedded in the sand, until they're unable pull any more.

Waiting for us is a large whaleboat and crew.

"Come on!" yells one of the men standing by the boat.

Jumping from the buggy, I struggle to run in the sand and fall. James quickly reaches down and helps me up. Pulling me in tow, he holds onto my hand, not letting go as we race across the beach to the boat.

I give little time remembering when I first arrived in Australia. I haven't been to the shore and felt the sand under my feet since I was a young girl. Felling the salty breeze on my face my heart pounds thinking about being free.

By the time we reach the rowboat, the crew is already shoving it out into the water. Wading out to climb aboard, James jumps in first, then reaches for my arms and pulls me into the boat, painfully raking the tops of my thighs on its wooden side. I don't care, all I want to do is get in.

Not knowing where I should sit, the crew tries to make room for me. It doesn't matter, I'm here, and I'm going! Gathering my skirt tightly in my arms, I climb past the oarsmen, to stow myself in the very front. The Fenians board and spread out, sitting among the rowers.

As we row away, I look back at the abandoned horses and buggies on the beach. How long before the guards realize we're gone? Well, not long. We're barely out from shore when I see several men on horses galloping towards the beach. They start shooting at us. But by now, we've rowed far enough for them not to hit us.

Staying quiet, I watch the chaos. The crew seems confused, perhaps questioning why someone would be shooting at us.

Then a loud voice yells to them. "I'll tell you all what's happening when we get to the ship. Now, pull men, row in time. You're all over the place."

I'm guessing the crew isn't used to anyone shooting at them.

One oarsman nods toward the man shouting orders and tells James, "That's the ship's captain. Captain Anthony."

Still having trouble getting the crew to work together, the captain yells, "Stay with your rowing men, or we'll go nowhere. Now Pull! Pull!" as his commands set the pace for his seamen.

These crewmen, with strong hands on their oars soon take on the rhythm and stay in time. I keep out of their way, I don't want them to have any reason to throw me overboard.

Several hours later, the weather starts to change. The surging waves get choppier and rain begins to fall. Through the noise, someone yells, "There are too many in the boat. We have to be careful, or we could take on too much water and sink. Anyone not rowing, bail water and dump it over the side."

I cup my hands, trying to help when someone grabs a pail from under the seats and hands it to me. Helping scoop for a few minutes, my arms get tired. But then, thankfully, the cloudburst stops.

The men row out to sea in the direction where the ship is to be waiting. I fall asleep for a little while, but then suddenly awake to the new roughness of the sea. *How far away is our ship?* The sun has set, and it's dark now. I can't see, but the men seem to know where they're going and continue to row. *Will we ever get there? Where's the ship?* I hold on tight as our small boat bobs on the waves. The men row all through the night

It starts to rain again, and the waves get rougher. I hold tight as the boat tosses on the waves. "Grab the pails again," someone yells. "We need to keep the water out. Hurry!"

Come sunrise, the cloud burst gets worse. The water is coming in faster than we can bail it out. Angry waves toss us around as if we're nothing, but still these amazing men keep us afloat and keep on rowing.

Finally, the rain stops, and I see the *Catalpa* in the distance. The wind makes the waves dangerously choppy, so it's hard to make any headway. We are still some distance away when one of the crew spots an approaching ship in the distance.

"Everyone get down," orders the captain.

Lying flat in the bottom of the boat isn't easy with so many of us. The captain says we need to appear as a floating log until the ship passes. Already low in the bow of the boat, I only have to scoot down and drop my head. Soon that ship moves past without noticing us.

The captain tells the crew, "It's probably the Royal Navy looking for us. We have to make it to our ship, or we'll all be put in irons. Any of the ships or boats we might see could be searching for us, so we need to do what we can to make sure they don't spot us."

The crew grumbles but obey his orders.

Seeing another ship passing on the horizon, one says, "That one won't bother us. We're too far away, and besides, its crew might not even see us."

Looking at our ship in the distance, I wish we were already there.

The captain looks at the *Catalpa* and says, "She's been waiting out in the deep waters, and it looks like the storm might have caused her to drag both her anchors. It seems she's been pushed farther out to sea. It won't be long now and we'll be aboard ship."

"Get down, a large steamer's passing off our bow. Shh! everyone quiet."

We all lie low, hoping not to be seen. I can hear the vessel chugging as it slowly moves past, not taking notice of our boat. The waves are still quite high, so we hope its crew won't be able to see us. I peek as it moves away, knowing it has to be searching for us.

Suddenly it turns back in our direction, apparently to investigate. As the steamer comes closer, we realize we've been spotted. We're still at quite a distance, but we hear someone shouting through a speaking-trumpet for us to stop. Everyone in our boat starts shouting, hurry, as our crew rows with all their strength. Then I hear shots firing. I keep down but hear a bullet zing past my head, scaring me I close my eyes and stay huddled in my safe place. They keep firing at us, but those bastards are terrible shots. We have quite a lead on them, plus the waves are still rough, making it hard to hit their target.

As we get closer to the *Catalpa*, I can't help but put my head up to see. Oh, we're almost there. The men look completely exhausted. I know I am, and I'm not doing anything but sitting here.

The steamer now heads straight for us. My heart pounds as the boat gets closer. I start to cry, fearing I might not survive our escape.

Captain shouts, "Row men! Row! Our life depends on it!"

At last we reach the *Catalpa*, and hurry to climb the rope ladder hanging over the side. Going up the ladder suddenly brings back memories I don't want to think about. Not good memories, that's for sure. Climbing down a rope ladder just like this one, so many years ago, took me into hell. But today, I'm climbing up to freedom. I grab on with everything I have inside me and pull myself on board.

But the danger isn't over. From a distance the heavily armed steamer fires off its small cannon, and a ball lands in the water near the front of the *Catalpa*.

Captain Anthony orders his crew, "Hoist anchor!"

I hear heavy chains pull the anchors from the sea bottom.

He gives another order. "Fly the colors, Mr. Smith."

"Aye, Captain!" A flag is raised on a pole off the back of the ship.

I look around at the crew and see they're armed and ready to fight. All the men from the rowboat quickly grab rifles. I know I would rather die than be taken back to prison, so I grab a long wooden peg to hit anyone who might try to take me. I feel like that little girl hiding in the shed again.

With no wind, our ship remains motionless on the water. Looking up at the massive sails, I see they hang flat. The ship is helplessly adrift, which makes us a sitting target for the steamer.

As the steamer chugs up alongside, our captain motions for us former prisoners to stay out of sight.

Huddling low beside the side rail, I hide. I hear everything. The two captains argue, exchanging some choice words. The captain of the steamer demands that the *Catalpa* return to Australia and surrender the prisoners.

"We have no prisoners on board, and everyone on this ship is free. Captain Anthony shakes his head "no," then points to the flag flying from the pole on the stern, one I've never seen before. Its colors are red, white, and blue, with stripes and stars. Looking back at the captain, I hear him say something about "International waters" and the "American flag." Again he points to the flag, vowing not to surrender, and tells them that they have no jurisdiction over his ship in these waters.

For the longest time, the steamer continues to bob on the waves in an attempt to block our escape. But then, a high wind begins to blow, filling our giant sails and pushing our ship forward. We nearly collide with the steamer before sailing into the vast open ocean, leaving the steamer and Australia behind.

This fight is over.

23

1876

I stand on the deck of the *Catalpa*, feeling stunned. Shaking and numb at the same time, I try to understand the magnitude of what has happened. My thoughts scramble as I take a deep breath. Is it really over? Smiling and breathing hard, tears start running down my face. I didn't think I'd make it. I thought I was going to die.

Looking over at James, I see him staring at me. He smiles, then walks over and takes me in his arms. I bury my face on his chest as he holds me tight. Sobbing from emotions that have been held prisoner inside me for so long, I cannot stop.

On the quarterdeck, two of the Fenians bend down and kiss the boots of the bearded man from the pier. It's a real gesture of their gratitude. Before long, all six men and myself, are thanking him and the captain for their heroic plan of escape. Our smiles and tears show overwhelming feelings that cannot be put into words.

Thomas comes over and hugs me, lifts me off my feet, and swings me around. Before long, the other Irishmen who didn't want me to come on this escape embrace me with hugs. James winks at me as the men slap his back and hug him too. We're happy to be free, and I'm a part of it all.

"Mr. Smith, call all hands on deck," says Captain Anthony.

"Aye, Captain."

Walking over, Mr. Smith rings a bell, and soon the entire crew gathers on deck, waiting to hear what the captain has to say.

121

"Men, I know you are confused as to what has taken place and why there are prisoners on board. The *Catalpa* was purchased for the sole purpose of rescuing these six Fenian prisoners from the Fremantle Prison. And the lady, well, she was a surprise. Mr. Breslin, Mr. Desmond, and I were hired by the Clan–na-Gael, an Irish group in New York, with plans for the rescue. No one on ship knew, except myself, until we ported in Australia. I then told Mr. Smith as we arrived, and he agreed to be a part of such a venture. I know the rowing crew were told that we were picking up passengers on the beach, but I didn't disclose they were prisoners. For this, I am sorry. Because of the secrecy of the mission, I could not reveal it to anyone. But I want to thank the crew for your bravery and dedication to duty. Our goal now is to take these men ... and the lady... safely to America. That will be all."

After hearing everything, I walk to the rail of the ship and try to reflect on what I'm feeling. I don't know…stunned, scared maybe. I look out at the ocean ahead, water that goes forever, so deep and blue. The sunlight glistens and dances on every wave, mesmerizing me. Frozen in time, I try to understand it all. How long will it be before I'll grasp my newfound freedom?

Feeling drained, I slide down on the deck and sit. Looking at the crew, I shiver from the unknown. Seeing the same kind of piercing eyes that I've seen at the prison, I feel worried.

Sensing my uneasiness, James comes and sits beside me. Taking my hand, he smiles.

"Adeleen, we have to be careful on ship, especially you. After hearing the Captain, I'm sure there will be mixed feelings among the crew. So maybe you should keep one of us Fenians in sight at all times. I don't want anything to happen to you."

Nodding, I feel better, knowing I have the six with me.

Standing, James and I gaze across the water towards the horizon. I can still see Australia far in the distance. We stand watching for what seems like forever, until we see it no more. Now it will be only a memory, an ugly memory that will probably visit me many times in nightmares. But over time maybe those, too, will fade, like the memory of the faces and voices of my mum and brother. Even my memories are cruel to me.

From across the deck, we hear orders. "Tighten the ropes! Mainsail, haul! Hoist them high! Pull till your guts spill out!"

Higher and higher another massive canvases rises, until the salty wind fills it to the full. I feel the ship lunge as it moves faster across the waters. It cuts straight through the waves like a sharp knife, and I'm grateful to be on board.

The sky is clear, not a cloud in it, and the air is clean and fresh. No longer do I have to breathe the evil stench of the prison. Letting the breeze cover my face, I take in a deep breath, filling my lungs with the fresh salty air as a free woman.

"Are you hungry, Miss?" a raspy voice asks me.

Smiling and looking over my shoulder, I see a man's weathered face with a big grin on it.

"Yes, I'm starved."

"They'll be serving something in the galley real soon, Miss. Just listen for the bell. I'm Samuel Smith, Captain's First Mate," he says, waiting for me to speak.

"Oh, I'm Adeleen Kelly. I'm pleased to meet you, Mr. Smith."

Immediately my thoughts go back to the prison, to the other Samuel I knew, and want to forget. Bringing myself back to the moment, I push my bad memories away.

"I've heard the captain say we're going to America and that it will take months to cross this giant ocean. Is that true?" I ask.

"Yes, Miss. It could take five or more months, but you'll find safety on American soil. There's no place like it," answers Mr. Smith.

Not knowing what questions to ask him about this America, I smile.

"That was quite something wasn't it?" he says. "Captain Anthony, he's a sharp one, you know. He'll stand up to anyone. He's American, you know, a real Yankee blue-blood. Of course, most of us crewmates are Yankees. Not all, but most."

Yankees? Curious what those are, but afraid to get in a long conversation, I think it best if I ask another time, when I'm not so hungry and tired.

I turn to look at this "Yankee" captain he's praising. My eyes follow him as he walks across the deck with a scruffy dog following behind. What's that, a dog on the ship? Well, that piques my interest!

"What's it like, here on the ship?" I ask Mr. Smith.

"What do you mean, Miss?"

"Well, is it safe?"

"There ain't not'in gonna happen to you, Miss. This ship is strong, and there are many a man on board sailing her. It'll take ya safely across the sea.

I study his leathery face and smile. "You must tell me about the dog. There must be a story."

Mr. Smith laughs. "Well, there's a story all right. He sure is an ugly, mangy-haired mutt, isn't he? We all call him Scraps."

How sad to have a name like Scraps.

"He belongs to the captain. The story has it the captain found him while he was ashore some years back. He found him starving, so he took him home, fed him, and the rest is what you see. The dog goes everywhere the captain goes. When the captain tried to leave the dog onshore when we set sail, the dog wouldn't stay. He jumped in the water and swam after the ship. There was nothing else to do but take him on board. He's been our ship dog ever since. He's no bother. We crew like him here. We give him our meal scraps, so that's what we call him. I've never asked the captain what his name is — he just calls him Dog."

I ask Mr. Smith, "Where does one go to use the privy?"

He laughs and says, "It's below deck, but we call it the 'head' on ship. It's towards the bow of the ship."

"Bow?"

"Yes, miss, that's the front of the ship."

Nodding, I move towards the stairs. Then hesitate while looking down the steps. I don't relish going below alone, but I don't have a choice. I'm surely not going to ask anyone to go with me. And I'm not going to call it "the head" either. That's barmy.

Before I take a step, a bell rings. Men aloft shimmy down from the mast, while others climb up. I chuckle to myself. It must be a change of crew. One man is holding onto the ropes with his hands and bare feet. I watch him climb high into the wind and sails. What are they doing up there so high? No time to watch now, I have to go.

Oil lamps hanging throughout give a dimly lit view of a large untidy room below deck. It's smelly and stuffy, with hammocks hanging from rafters. I see a few men trying to sleep, so I tiptoe past. There's a table in the middle of it all, where some of the crew are gathered talking and smoking their pipes. They nod and keep their eyes on me as I pass by. One of the crew points in the direction I need to go, then smiles. How does he know?

The air below is most suffocating from their pipe smoke, but it isn't anything like the stench of the ship that took me to Australia. I can deal with this. After all, I'm just grateful to be on board.

After visiting the privy, I take a different route to go up top. I pass by the galley, stopping to peek in and see a short fat man busy fixing the meals. Not wanting to interrupt him, I say nothing. I think it best if I wait to be introduced. I don't know what kind of a man he is, nor do I want to find out while I'm alone.

Back up on deck, I join my group of Fenians, who are sprawling out in the sun. Smelling the cooking coming from the galley below, I'm happy I don't have to cook it. Ha, ha, I laugh to myself, but my stomach growls to remind me that I've eaten very little in days. Anything will taste good.

Then the bell rings again, signaling time to eat. As we make our way to the steps that lead below, I hear some of the crew following behind, shoving one another to get closer to us. They're a curious lot, and even though nobody told them this voyage was a rescue mission, some are excited we're on board.

James tells me how some of the crew might feel about being shot at during our escape and what they might think about having a woman on board. He says some of the crew may look at the rescue as a victory they won because of the standoff. A few of them might even be running from the law themselves, or something else in their life. So, to be able to raise their fist and stand in defiance and strong must have been liberating for them. Others, though, might have different feelings. They had signed on to whale, and probably feel betrayed.

"The fact that you're on board, Adeleen, probably adds to their dislike," James tells me. "Some sailors don't like women on a ship. They might even think they bring bad luck."

Hearing this, all I know is I'll feel safer if I stay close to my six while on this voyage.

As we make our way to the galley below, we are greeted by the cook. He smiles at us, and beckons us to come in.

"There ain't nobody can remember me real name. I'm Peatronilli and was born in Italy. You's can call me Peat or Cook, or whatever you want. It makes a no matter to me. I'll answer."

Chuckling at his introduction, we all smile and move closer to the food.

"You new ones, you hungry?" he asks.

"Yes," we answer in unison, as we look at each other, nodding in agreement.

"We're starved," I reply.

Handing a plate to me, Cook scoops in a big ladle of chunky salt beef stew, then gives me a spoon. A spoon, a real spoon. We get to eat with a metal spoon, unlike the wooden carved ones we had to use at the prison. I smile at James, and he nods and smiles back.

As I lean over to smell my dish, Peat says, "Might not be as good as you think, Miss."

"Miss." How that word resonates in my ears. "Oh no, it smells wonderful. I'll wager it tastes just as good as it smells too," I say as I start to gobble it. I'm sure I'm not very lady-like about the way I'm eating right now, but I'm hungry, and I can be a lady another time. We're all hungry. He has no idea what we've been through, and the last meal any of us had was almost two days ago at the prison.

"Mmm"…I moan as I enjoy every bite. Peat looks at me with his big smile and scoops more onto my plate.

"Oh!"…I'm so sick. Soon, what is in my stomach is there no longer as I lose it over the side of the ship. Collapsing onto the deck, a hopeless feeling comes over me. *What's happening to me?* Across the deck, a few of the crew laugh, watching me as I repeatedly spew my meal into the ocean. It is clear they know that feeling. You almost can't be on a ship rocking up-and-down, and side-to-side, with a full

126

stomach, and not feel some sickness the first few days. It will take me some time, but they know I'll be fine.

"Want a blanket, Miss?" a friendly voice asks.

I look up and see Mr. Smith. I nod my head yes, as he hands it to me. "Thanks. You're so kind, Mr. Smith," I whisper.

Wrapping it around my shoulders, I return to my thoughts, but those thoughts overwhelm me. Is my freedom real? Why do I feel so lost? Is it just the new feelings I have without walls, without guards, and without restraints? It's all so scary. Have I done the right thing by leaving? The prison has left me with deep wounds that someday, I pray, will scar over.

My mind swims. I want to unburden myself from all the bad, horrible, cruel things I did in prison. I almost feel like my heart has turned to stone. I want to be alive again. Crying, I bury my face in my hands. Will I ever be able to let go of all this ugliness? What if it never goes away?

Suddenly, I feel the ship lifting high up on the waves as it heads across the water, and peace floods over me as my soul begins to open. Is this freedom coming in? I know, somehow, I'll find my new life, whatever it might be. Sitting very still, I don't dare move for fear of losing my thoughts. Staying quiet and letting the ship carry me away, for a moment I think I might be starting to find myself.

"Adeleen," calls a familiar voice. "Are you feeling better?" ask James.

"Maybe a little," I say, smiling back at him.

"You'll feel better. It takes time to get used to the movement of the ship."

"Wasn't that something?" James excitedly re-living the standoff between the two ships. "They just backed off. They didn't dare board our ship! What a feeling. I've never seen anything like it. Ha, ha, they couldn't do a thing!"

Hearing our laughter, two more of the Fenians, Michael and Robert, come over to join in.

"Yes, it's hard to believe we're all free," I say.

Looking at them, I see how happy they are. Before long, we're all together again, and I feel safe.

As the sun begins to set over the water, the sky is pink, and the laughter on the ship turns to music as the crew brings out their instruments. Some of the men dance and sing with joy. They're telling stories and singing, songs of old and songs a new. Not all join in; those crewmen stayed below. But for us on deck, we want to celebrate.

Laughing, we watch as one of the crew climbs high to the top of the mast and removes the green streamer. Climbing back down, he walks over to me and ties it around my waist. My stomach is still churning somewhat, and I'm feeling weak, but nothing is going to stop me from enjoying the gala. The fun of it all is something to behold. I smile as some are wanting to dance with me. I am free to enjoy, free to live, though still a little sick, but oh so happy.

The ship takes on a peaceful quietness after the celebration. Just a few feet away, James and the others sprawl on the deck to sleep. The day is gone, and the waters have turned to the color of slate as the sky darkens. Looking up at the full moon and stars, then back at the waves capturing their light, I'm lost in a trance as the sea again draws my thoughts. Where do I go? What will I do? My life ahead seems so open. Still have so many questions and no answers. Maybe I'm just afraid of the unknown.

Looking out over the waves, a chill from a cooling breeze blows over me, and I soon find myself curled up in a corner on deck. Continuing to stare at the vast openness of the water, I pull my blanket up over my shoulders. The sky is full of millions of bright stars, some shooting across it. I feel like reaching up and touching them all. They must be shining down on me as if to say, *"You're safe now."* I sit there, so exhausted from everything.

Soon the rocking rhythm and the sound of the waves caressing the sides of the ship begin to lull me towards sleep, but I fight it. I'm afraid if I fall asleep, I'll wake up to find it was all a dream, and I'll be back in Hell again.

"She'll rock you to sleep," says a voice.

Seeing Samuel's friendly face, he tells me, "This ship — she'll rock you to sleep. Just let her." He smiles again as he walks past, testing the tension of the ropes.

Chuckling, I lean back against the ship. Listening to the waves lapping against her wooden hull, I soon close my eyes, giving in to its gentle rocking.

24

Never do I remember sleeping so peacefully. Maybe it was rocking of the ship, exhaustion, or my feelings of being safe. I awake to blue skies above and a cool morning breeze. It's a peaceful morning, my first away from the dirty, smelly, hellish prison.

As I lie on the deck looking up, I see the massive sails above and hear the creaking sounds of the numerous ropes stretching as the giant sails billow in the wind. Staying quiet and taking it all in, I don't want to move. But, when I finally sit up, I see the crew already busy climbing among the riggings making adjustments to the ropes. Someone told me each rope has a name. How strange. Maybe they name them after their women back at home.

Up on the bridge, Captain Anthony is giving orders to his crew. I watch as the men pull ropes to hoist another giant sail. It's all so breathtaking.

"Morning, Miss," says one of the crew as he walks past.

Startled, I nod as I reach up and try to tame my windblown red hair and find I'm still wearing my wooden comb that Mychael gave me. I gasp, ever so grateful I haven't lost it — it's the only good thing I have to remember about my friends at the prison.

With the sun shining brightly in the sky, another crewman nods and says, "Morning, Miss," to welcome me to the new day on the ship. This, too, is so new to me, to be called Miss and greeted so respectfully. I feel so unworthy but so grateful.

The deck is a bustle of activity. As I walk over to my group from the prison, I see Mr. Smith. His sun-dried face carries a smile as he approaches us.

James asks, "Mr. Smith, do you have time to tell us something about the ship and the crew?"

"What do you want to know?" questions Mr. Smith.

Listening to Mr. Smith's strange accent, I can't help but smile. Is that the way everyone talks in America?

"There's quite a lot of men on this ship. What do they all do?" James adds.

Stroking his chin for a moment, Mr. Smith says, "Yes, I can tell you. Let me think now...let's see." Pointing to a few of the men, he shares how the ship is manned.

"Well, this here's a whaling ship. We travel the waters to hunt for the big fish. The biggest there is in the ocean, the whale. It takes a good lot of men with different skills to do what we do. It's a tough, rough life, one that is exciting and terrifying at the same time. To tell you the truth, like Captain told us, the crew didn't know we were coming to rescue you until you climbed on board. He shared that with me when we docked in Fremantle, but we told no one else. It was a surprise to us all, except him. He kept his mission a secret all along. You must be grateful for the rich Irish men from America who planned this whole escape for you all."

Mr. Smith continues. "Each man knows his duties. Starting first, of course, there's the captain. He runs this ship, and his word is law, even if we don't like it. He has the final say so, and if he tells you to do something, you best do it. Then next in command is me. I'm the captain's First Mate. If the captain 's busy or off the ship, I'm in charge. Not boasting. It's a fact," he tells us.

Mm-hmm, he's boasting.

"Then there's Brady, over there," he says, pointing to a slender man checking the ropes. "He's Second Mate. Let's see now. We have the boatsteerers, Riley and Jackson. They ride the waves in the rowboats chasing the whale, then harpoon it for the kill. They have to have a good aim to do that job. We also use them to help move the giant melting pots when it comes time to render the blubber. They're the strongest two men on ship. The boatsteerers have more responsibilities and get paid more money when we get a whale. Sims and Cully, and eight others who are probably below deck, are oarsmen. You saw them in the whaleboat that brought you to the ship. We have quite a few of them. We need them to row when we chase the whale. They, too, have to be mighty strong."

Following Mr. Smith on deck, we are eager to hear more.

"That there lad," he says pointing to the youngest of the crew, "his name's Christian, the captain's cabin boy. He's 19 years and no longer a boy, but Captain likes him and doesn't want to train another youngster to take his place. But Christian's been sailing for, maybe, five years. Probably next trip, he'll be promoted.

"There's many more men, about twenty-five in all. A few are greenhorns, which means they've never sailed before and have to learn. But, for the most, the crew is good. Not a large crew for a ship our size."

James stands and looks up at the crewmen working the lines and sails. I wager he's wondering if he has the nerve to climb the heights like them. As for me, I'll just watch.

As I walk towards the back of the ship, my eyes capture the flag flying in the breeze off the back of the ship. Stopping and standing quiet, I take a long look at it as it waves in the wind. As one of the crewmen walks past, I say, "Thirty-seven."

"What?" asks the crewmen?

"I counted them. There are thirty-seven stars on that flag."

"Yes, Miss, that's the American flag. Captain bought us a nice new one to fly for this voyage. There's a star for every state in the Union, you know."

"No, I'm not aware of what the flag means. Tell me more."

He walks closer. "My name is Stewart," he tells me.

"I'm Adeleen."

"I know. I hear the men when they call your name. It's a pretty name,"

Is he flirting? "I don't know anything about America, but I hear that's where we're going."

"Yes, Miss, it is," he replies with a big grin. Looking up at the flag with pride, he tells me, "We have more states joining all the time. Our country is so big, and there is so much land out west, a person can plant themselves anywhere and be happy."

Smiling, I ask, "Have you been to America?"

Chuckling, he says, "Yes, Miss, it's my home. You'll like it." Then he moves on to continue his work.

Hmm, he has that Yankee accent too.

Across the deck, I'm aware of some of the men staring at me. They're going about their tasks haphazardly, all the while keeping their eyes fixed on me. I'm used to being watched at the prison, but this is different. This crew doesn't know me, and I don't know them. I notice some of the men turn away when I look at them, but a few others glare back. I'm getting a sense of a different kind of danger on board, one that gives me chills. Are there ghosts here too?

"Adeleen, here you are. I have some coffee for you."

It's James, attempting to hand me a hot mug. I laugh as he sways with the motion of the ship. He's a little unsteady but manages to keep from spilling it.

"They even have molasses to sweeten it," James tells me with a big smile. "It's going to take a little time to get me seafaring legs, though."

Reaching for the mug, I ask, "What do you think we should be doing?"

"Aye, I hope to find out soon."

Sipping my coffee, I stop and take a deep breath. "James, I want to tell you something."

"Aye, Adeleen, but we'll have to talk later," he says, smiling as he hurries off, no doubt to tell the others about the molasses for the coffee. The men had slept on deck close to the stairwell, so when the aroma of the coffee seeps up from the galley, it wakes them. It's not long before we're all together, laughing, and discussing our lives ahead.

James forgot I wanted to talk to him, but I'd rather tell him in private. Before long, we're all sitting together enjoying our freedom. Two of the men, Martin and Robert, sit quietly, as if they're in shock. It's been years since these men have gathered and laughed together.

They look worn from the abuse and torture they've had to endure through the years. Their faces look haunted and hardened with lines and scars.

Reaching up, I touch my own face. What has prison it done to me?

One of the crew walks over and leans down and whispers something in James's ear. He gets up and follows him to where Captain Anthony is standing on the upper deck.

Soon James comes back. "The captain wants to meet with us after we settle and have our morning meal."

The smell of cooking below in the galley changes my thoughts. Ugh, I'm not sure if I want to eat again after what happened yesterday. But it does smell good. Maybe I shouldn't be such a pig this time.

Finally, we hear the bell ringing for chow. The six Irishmen are so eager to go below that they almost trample over each other. Then they remember...me.

"After you, your Majesty," they say as they bow and give way.

Smiling, I savor the moment. Never has this ever happened. These men are treating me like a lady. As I step down the first step, I hear them joking behind as they climb over one another trying to be next. All this laughter is contagious, and I'm so happy.

<hr/>

Well, later never happened. I guess what I want to tell James will have to wait for another time, but I'll need to build my nerve again before I do.

After our morning meal, we climb up the steps back onto the deck. Captain Anthony and his First Mate, Mr. Smith, walk over to meet with our group. The captain explains why he had been so late for our rescue and the difficulties they had encountered at sea. He assures us that within six months, or sooner, we will reach America. Until then, we're free to join the crew and help anytime, or relax and enjoy our new freedom. Tipping his hat, he says he is glad we're on board.

Not wanting to take my eyes off this handsome captain, I watch him walk back to the upper deck. He stands so tall, so straight. What strength he portrays. To think he guided this ship across the vast ocean waters taking us out of danger to a better life. What does that take? Confidence, knowledge, courage? I shake my head as the thought overwhelms me. To think he came only for us…well maybe not me. I'm an extra. But it must have been all so dangerous. To cross the ocean is dangerous enough, but to actually break us out of prison — that's a masterpiece.

❧❧❧❧❧

As the days go by, the winds begin to blow harder, moving our ship faster across the water. The winds are steady at first and then grow stronger as gales push us as if we are in a race. The waves lift the ship high, only to crash down again with great force. *Exciting!*

Holding tight onto the side rail, I carefully make my way across deck, where animals are kept in cages. There are chickens, rabbits, and, tied on a rope that's tethered to a ring bolted to the deck is a goat. The chickens are for their eggs, and the goat for its milk, and other small animals…well.

Sitting down among them, I pet the goat. "I'm sorry you're all tied up — I know exactly how you feel. Don't worry. You'll be free soon when we get to America. Maybe I can take you home with me, wherever that might be."

Checking the chickens, I notice some have laid eggs. I smile, "I see you're all doing your job. Keep up the good work. There are a lot of hungry men on board."

Looking beyond the cages, I see harpoons in a neat pile. I walk over and touch the end of one of the sharp iron spears. I know nothing about whaling and wonder if these spears are what they use, or maybe they use these to fight off the giant sea monsters that I've heard stories about.

Breathing out a big sigh, I realize there is so much of life I don't know and understand. All I know is the prison, and nothing of the real world, or life.

25

We're well into the sixth day when the bell rings, signaling all hands that a storm is coming. There are certain rhythms to the bells. Each ring has a different meaning. The captain yells orders as each man knows his duty, with no confusion. Everyone works together, focusing on tasks to secure the ship before the storm hits.

This is my first storm at sea on the *Catalpa*, and I'm excited. One of the crew asks me if I will help gather up the smaller things on deck that might wash overboard and take them below. I nod yes and reach out to grab a bucket as it starts to slide across the deck when the ship begins to pitch from the large waves. Enjoying the challenge, while trying to stand without falling, I have fun grabbing items before they slide out of my reach. Gathering what I can, I carry them to store safely below.

The crew, high on the mast, are singing. Maybe they're just showing off for me. But watching, I soon understand. They're singing to stay in a steady rhythm while moving the giant sails. I'm in awe and start to feel love for sailing.

"Where there's wind, there are big waves," a crewman says as he smiles at me.

Holding on tight to the rail, I feel the mighty wind as it blows us across the water, and sure enough, the stronger it gets, the higher the waves, just like he says.

Mr. Smith tells me that this time of year, the squalls might come in one on top of another, making navigation difficult. When we left, Australia was going into winter, and now America is going into summer. We are caught somewhere in between, and the gales testify to that.

"It's like the world's all mixed-up and doesn't know what to do," he says.

Tonight's darkness covers the stars, so they must rely on a compass alone. The ship's chronometer, which helps navigate, is still broken, so it's all up to the captain. I sit and watch this skillful man standing on the upper deck, yelling out orders, and his crew obeying his every word. He's amazing.

As with all storms, a ship is at the mercy of the winds, waves, and currents. The cold, salty spray increases as the waves break over the deck and the water gets rougher. It blows harder, and soon becomes brutal. The wind screams through the riggings, like it wants to tear everything down. The thunder rumbles from across the water, moving closer with every gust.

The man at the helm on the quarterdeck struggles to hang onto the ship's wheel. Captain makes his way over and reaches out to help hold it while two crewmen secure it with a rope. If they should lose their grip, the ship might careen out of control and tip, causing it to break apart.

Lightning splits the sky as it rips through the clouds — thunder exploding overhead as we move into the storm. The wind gusts toss our ship like small stick floating on water. Mr. Smith points to the dark clouds and tells me that the captain has tried to skirt the ship around the storm, but to no avail its winds are blowing straight at us. We have no choice but to go into it.

A brave crewman climbs the masts to secure a sail that's torn loose as the winds howl and scream. Looking at the angry waters, I have a sense of its infinite depth, and I'm frightened. I remember the ship taking me to Australia rocked violently, but I was below and didn't know of the danger.

"A real storm is coming," says Stewart as he looks up at the sky, "She'll blow real hard soon."

Soon? Do you mean to tell me it's going to get worse?

Looking in the direction we're traveling, fear grips my insides. Ahead I see a monstrous dark wall of clouds that goes from heaven to water. As we get closer, the spray becomes rain. Our ship rises on every wave, then comes crashing down with a great moan as the saltwater makes its way over the deck.

"You'd best find a safe place below, Miss," a voice says.

Looking around for something to grab tightly onto as the ship pitches, I'm afraid and feel lost. I don't know where to go to be safe. Holding on the best I can, I stay where I am for fear of being swept overboard.

The rain becomes colder and starts to sting as the dart-like drops strike my face. I don't know what I should do. I'm too afraid to go below, and too scared to stay topside.

"Bloody hell, Adeleen! What are you still doing up here?"

It's James. He reaches out, and I grab onto his hand. Pulling me along with him, he takes me to the stairs that lead below. I let go and sit in the opening to watch the storm.

The winds rip at our sails and churn the rough seas. Minutes seem like hours as we dare to fight the storm. This ship that I thought so big has become small on these massive waves. I hear the bell ringing with every tilt, and see the crew looking up at the three tall masts and ropes, praying nothing will rip or snap. Some sails are tightly rolled, ready from the storm, while others take it on. The height and weight make the masts seem like they're giant swords dueling with the wind as lightning bolts strike the sky. The massive masts creak as in agony, giving me the fear they will break and fall. What will happen if they do?

No! She's going to hold together. Much like me, she has fight in her and won't fail. Sometimes we can't go around things that make us afraid — we have to go through them. So here I stay in the doorway that leads below.

Today I stay strong and realize this is only the beginning for me on the high seas as our ship travels to the far side of the world to carry me on my grand adventure to freedom.

Here I sit testing my nerve, and knowing this will probably happen over and over again with this great ocean.

26

Over the next few days the winds lessen, but, the rain continues to pound. Most of the crew are kind to me, but others keep their distance, giving me an uneasy feeling. I have been given a place to sleep below deck, away from the changing weather. A few of the crew have rigged a curtain around a hammock that hangs from rafters. This is something new; I have never tried to sleep in one. Just getting in it is a problem. The crew laughs every time I get in, only to hear me being tossed out.

Over and over again, I attempt to conquer the hammock, but with the rocking of the ship and my inability to understand the bloody thing, I soon decide to sleep on the floor. It isn't so bad. I figure over time I can scavenger up something more to cushion my bed. All I know is, I don't want to swing in one of those blasted things all night. At least I'm warm, dry, and safe, and that's just fine with me. I just hope if there are rats on ship, they leave me alone.

The storm has finally passed, and the visibility is unlimited across the water and blue skies. The winds blow steadily, moving our ship across the waves to carry me to my new home.

Twice a day Captain Anthony walks the entire ship. This noble-looking man often slows and smiles at me when he and his dog pass. I think he might be pleased to see a female among all the men. Smiling to myself, I start to go down the stairwell when I overhear angry voices talking. Stopping and backing against the wall, I stay hidden from their sight and listen.

"We come on this ship to whale."

"Aye, we're whalers," voices another.

"To hell with all this rescue stuff. Our captain lied to us. The law will probably be upon us at the next port, and then they'll be all over our ship. I don't like it," another says.

"Yea, he's right. It'll just be a matter of time, and then they'll find us too."

"And what about her? She's a devil woman. We know she's bad luck for our ship. She has to go."

"Send her under," another yells.

"Quiet, they'll hear us!"

"What can we do?"

"They ain't not'in we can do. We're stuck with 'em," grumbles another.

"They ain't hurt'n us, I like 'em," says another. "I'm glad we could help them get loose from prison."

"Aye," voices another.

"It'll be all right. It don't matter much to me. Let's just do our jobs and shut the hell up about it."

"You wenches whine all you want. I'm glad we rescued 'em. I wouldn't wanna been where they were. 'Tis a good thing we got 'em. Too bad we didn't get more."

Grumbling, the group slowly cools and breaks apart.

I quickly move back up on deck away from the stairwell as some of the men come up top.

Feeling uncomfortable, I'm now noticing glares from more of the men. Knowing a few of them don't want me here, like in prison, my thoughts turn to survival as I sense danger. I scan the crew many times, trying to remember who those men were that I overheard, although I only got to see the ones who came up the steps. Who are the others? I don't know who defended me or who wishes me gone. Should I tell James, or will that cause quarreling?

Two crewmen, Wylie and Drissel, walk slowly towards me with their eyes fixed on me. What are they up too? Having a gut feeling, I take a deep breath, bracing myself.

From my left, I hear Michael's voice. "Hey, Adeleen, there you are," he says. "James's wants you to join us," pointing across the deck to where he and Samuel are talking.

Still watching Wylie and Drissel, I see them divert their path and continue in another direction. Thank God for Michael walking up when he did. Or am I just imagining the danger?

Tonight there's a ghostly, smoke-like mist hovering over the water. The fog gets worse as our ship moves west across the Indian Ocean. Standing on the deck with James and the others, I've gazed at it so long I feel I might become blind. Feeling its dampness chill me, I wrap my blanket tightly around my shoulders, wishing it would all go away.

"The captain can pinpoint his course through this white hell. He knows how to sail this ship with his eyes closed. Don't be frightened, Miss, it's true. He'll take us through safely," says the night watchman.

Smiling, I give him a nod. Feeling a little safer, I make my way below to my bed.

I try to scream, but someone's holding me down with his hand over my mouth. Sweat rolls off my face as I kick, trying to free myself. My demons are back. Scratching, kicking, and screaming…I awake!

Frightened, my heart pounds, then I realize it's only my recurring nightmare. Breathing rapidly, my eyes scan my surroundings with fear. Pulling my blanket tightly, I curl into a ball and start to sob.

My screams must have been heard by most on ship. Before I know it, the crew have jumped from their hammocks, trying to find out what's wrong.

James pushes his way through the men to reach me. Kneeling by my side, he helps me to sit.

"She's all right. You can all go back to your berths. She's just having a bad dream."

He knows and understands. Seeing my distress, he cradles me in his arms. "Mind if I stay with you for a little while?" James asks.

Thankful he doesn't want to leave me, I cling to him.

He's witnessed the rapes at the prison. Not mine, but others'. So he knows the horror that's torturing my mind.

"How will I ever get over these nightmares?" I ask, trembling.

"I think you will," he says, trying to give me hope.

Hell, he doesn't know, he has his own demons. The guards had their special ways of abusing the men. They raped some of them too, so I've heard, but it was more for the guards' evil entertainment.

"I need some fresh air. Will you take me up on deck?"

"Aye," he says, helping me to my feet.

The fog has gone, and the sky is full of millions of stars. As James and I stand staring out at the water glistening in the moonlight, we look for answers. Together we try to push away the horrors of our past. With tears flowing without restraint down my face, I'm sorry for all the bad things I've done. The years of hurt, hatred, and pain start to empty.

I bury my face on his shoulder and cry until there are no tears left. Holding tightly onto his arm, I almost feel he's at a loss to know what to do. I lean closer, giving him the chance to put both arms around me, and finally, he does. Just being in the comfort of his embrace is enough. I want to stay here and feel safe, never to move. Giving out a deep sigh, I hold him close.

<hr />

The skies are blue and clear. We've been sailing for a month, and all the days seem to blend into one another. Still, we have a long way to sail, and the men are starting to get restless, with tensions beginning to build. Not all, but a few of the crew are starting to loudly voice their dislike of us being on board, making sure we hear. The endless days of sailing with nothing to keep anyone busy is turning out to be difficult on everyone.

High above in the masthead, a man stands on the crosstree keeping watch with a spyglass, scanning the water for the next big kill. This is a whaling ship, and these men need to whale.

Backing up against a deck wall, I slide down and sit. There's nowhere to feel safe. There are no shadows where I can hide. With mixed emotions, I start to feel like I'm in prison again, and I'm afraid. Soon my thoughts return to that dark place. How many that I left behind suffered the wrath from our prison break? Always before, when someone would try to escape, the guards would do a search of the whole prison trying to link anyone they could to punish. Even if you had nothing to do with it, the guards would make up some story to cover their sloppiness. I wish the whole place would burn with fire. It's such an evil place. I close my eyes and shudder.

What will become of my friends, Orla, Rou, Liz, and Sarah? I even think of Emma. Even though she's dead, I will never forget her. I didn't tell any of the girls what I was planning, so how would they know? Will they hear I made it to freedom, or will the guards make up some story and say we were all killed during the prison break? That's their way to teach others that if they are planning an escape, they too will find themselves dead. Sadly, too many are afraid to try.

✿✿✿✿✿

It's another beautiful morning, and the ocean is calm. Walking across the deck, the captain stops and puts out his hand, requesting mine. "Would you come with me, Miss?"

Not knowing why, I take his hand. Walking with him to the stern of the ship, we step up three steps to the door of his stateroom. I freeze as my heart begins to pound. Starting to shake, I feel the same fear I encountered in the prison when a guard ordered me to follow them.

Standing at the door, I gaze inside. I can actually smell the warmth of the beautiful wood carved room. Magnificent! From the glow of light coming in through the small windows, I see the captain's cabin with a stately bed.

Sensing my hesitation, he says, "No need to be frightened, Miss. I can leave the door open. I have something for you." He points to an old steamer trunk.

"What is it?" I nervously ask.

"This trunk was left on board from the last commander of this ship, Captain Wittman," he sadly tells me. "His wife died in childbirth

143

some years back, and he couldn't bring to rid himself of it, so he left it on board. It's been here ever since. I think you will find some of the things you might need in it. Take what you will or take it all."

My eyes widen as I lift the lid. Inside are all sorts of beautiful dresses, shoes, cloaks, and much more.

"Oh, Captain, I have never had such beautiful things. How can I ever thank you?"

"There's no need to thank me, Miss. I have no use for them, but I couldn't bear to throw them away. I knew someday I would find someone who would like them. They are yours. I'll leave you be to find what you like." With that, he closes the door behind him.

They're all so beautiful. I have never even touched things this lovely. I run my hand across the dresses feeling the delicate material. As I pull the first dress from the trunk, I understand my life is changing for the good. For a time I try on dresses, some over and over again, and they fit perfectly. I want to wear them all.

There are even shoes. Real ladies' shoes. Quite different from my boots I'm wearing. It's a miracle, just a downright miracle. I whirl and twirl, pull my hair up, and giggle at my new self. Now, this is going to take some getting used to, I thought, as I try to walk across the floor in the shoes. Wobbly, but I know over time, maybe I'll be able to get used to them.

Finally, I choose one — the pretty dark blue dress, the same color as the beautiful blue ocean that I'm traveling across to take me to my new life. I stand in front of a mirror and see someone I have never seen before...someone I like. Then I remember, like in prison, someone had to die to give me my clothes and shoes. I look down at my dirty, ragged clothes on the floor and kick them. Starting to cry, I think of all the sick, ugly things inside me, ugly stuff I want to leave on the floor with those rags. That's where it all belongs.

My tears start to flow and won't stop. I grab my new clothes and hug them tight, throwing myself on the bed. I have a new beginning, a real chance at life. Overwhelmed with emotions, I cling to my new clothes. Everything is going to be all right, I say to myself.

Again, I kick at the dirty clothes on the floor and look at them with disgust. Then I remember the girls — my friends I left behind and how hard and horrible their lives still are.

Sadness engulfs me, feeling regret that I had to leave them all behind. How can I be happy?

Grieving for them, I bury my face in my beautiful new clothes and cry even harder.

Whistles, non-stop whistles, greet me as I step onto the deck wearing my new dress. Smiles, whoops, and hollers from most all, with a grin on every one of their faces, including mine. I see James whistling and clapping as the others join with approval.

Busy at the helm, the captain looks over at me then nods with approval. Stepping down, he walks over and puts out his arm to escort me. I reach out and take it, and together we walk the deck. I feel like a lady, I say to myself, a real lady!

I notice the captain looking down at my bare feet, and then looking away. That's all right. I'll wear the shoes another day. Today, I just want the pretty blue dress.

27

Sailing high on the waves, the ship leaves a ribbon of wakes following behind. It's such a beautiful sight. How many days have we been sailing? -I don't know. I lost count. How much longer will it be before we get there? I think the crew gets tired of me asking, so I keep it to myself.

Feeling the breeze getting warmer, Samuel tells me it's a sure sign we are close to the tip of Africa. It's somewhere they call the Cape, whatever that is. It's a place where the waters are very turbulent, he tells me. But, for now, every wave shimmers in the sun as gusts blow across the blue-green waters. He says it's going to get quite hot when we go north to cross into the South Atlantic and over the equator.

"Really, will I be able to see it?"

Laughing, he says, "Oh, you'll know when we get there. It's going to be hellishly hot."

Wonderful. I'm looking forward to that event.

I'm in a rose-colored dress today, but with the sweltering heat, it's hard to be comfortable. I chose this dress today for my baby Rose and because it also reminds me of my mum's beautiful flowers at my home in England. I'm taking this day to remember them both.

I don't have many memories of my daughter, but I loved her so. I will forever cherish in my heart the memories of how I carried her inside me and feeling her move, and the short time I got to hold her before they took her away.

Thinking about my mum brings a smile to my face. She was a beautiful Irish woman with long, fiery red hair like mine. She was well educated, coming from a good family. My brother Benjamin is older than myself, but I remember his sandy red hair.

We had different fathers, Benjamin and me. Mum married Benjamin's father against her family's wishes when they were very young, and a year later, Benjamin was born. His father was an Irishman and well-liked by everyone in our neighborhood. Like many of the men in town, he worked in the coal mines. I was told it was a good living that provided for them.

He died one day when the mine caved in, crushing him and many others. They were able to bring him out of the tunnel, but he died a few days later. Mum's parents had died long ago and had disowned her, so it became very difficult for her to scrape out a meager living.

It wasn't until three years later that my mum met the wealthy man. He saw her in the marketplace one day and was captivated by her beauty. He came every day looking for her, and before long, they found ways to be together. There was just one problem — well, maybe two or three. She was poor and not of his class, and she was Irish, which was a big no, and he was married.

But they wanted to be with each other, so they had to be discreet and not be seen in public. He provided a small home for her and Benjamin, and only came to see her behind closed doors. So, that's how my mum survived in a difficult world. And then I came to be.

I have plenty of time to think of them as I sit around doing nothing. My thoughts of my mum and Benjamin give me comfort, but it's getting harder and harder to remember what they look like. Their faces are starting to fade, and it's hard to hear their voices in my thoughts. They're just getting further and further away in my memory.

Suddenly, I feel an icy cold fear come over me. I remember something that I had forgotten. Benjamin's father's name was Howard Cooper. At birth, I was given my mum's maiden name of Kelly. Frightened, I look back toward Australia. Coop? That's what the guards called the red-headed man in the hospital care room. Was that Benjamin I left behind? Dear God!

My heart rips, taking me into a deep pain I want no comfort from. One more time, the prison cuts deep into me.

For the next few hours, I stay away from anyone who tries to find out what's bothering me. I can't bring myself to tell them. I wave them away and crawl into myself. I find no comfort and don't want any. I vow this will be the last time the prison will ever hurt me. I want to be left alone. I just want to grieve.

I hear the others ask James, "What's wrong with Adeleen?"

"I don't know. She's in a prickly mood today, not wanting to be around anyone. She won't say what's bothering her."

I know the six care what's happening to me, but it isn't easy for me to think I came so close to finding Benjamin. Was I too wrapped up in myself that I didn't stay to find out? Why didn't I remember the name, Cooper? I might have had a better chance to know it was him if I had only remembered his last name.

Did he ever try to find me? Maybe he didn't know I was at the prison.

Again, the prison they call The Establishment has ripped me to my core. I don't think I'll ever stop hating that place. Hate is such a small word for what I feel. It's a lost feeling. Still, I wonder. If I had found out it was Benjamin after all, would I still have left with the six?

"The coffee's still hot. Want some?" asks James.

Thinking I don't want to hurt anymore, I know I have to let go to heal. Looking off the back of the ship towards Australia, I lower my head and whisper goodbye to Benjamin, then turn and look away. I have a choice and a chance. I need to take hold of it. I sure as hell can't swim back to Australia.

"Aye, I'll have that coffee," I say and reach out to take it.

Sipping my coffee, I find myself looking at the reflecting water. I get tired of always staring at it. Still, when I do, I have a sense of how small I am, how insignificant my life is with no reason for it. What will my new life be like? Will I feel alive again?

Trying to hold my emotions together I walk to the stern of the ship away from the men. I don't want any of them to see how much I'm struggling.

148

The heat is almost unbearable. As I fan myself, the midmorning sun begins to scorch our ship, and I'm told it will only get hotter as the day goes on. The men are working without their shirts, while I'm stuck wearing a heavy gown trying to look like a lady. My dress may be beautiful, but it's not made for the hot weather. Maybe looking deeper in the trunk I can find something that will be more comfortable.

As I climb the three steps heading to the captain's room, I nod to Captain Anthony, telling him I'm going to his cabin to change. I see him smile and nod in return, touching the tip of his hat. Momentarily, I'm smitten by his gallant gesture. Taking a deep breath, I hope my sudden attraction is not apparent by the flush of my cheeks. With luck, he'll think I'm just overheated. Reaching for the door, I dash inside.

Looking down into the trunk, I find a pair of strange looking breeches with soft leather sewn inside the thighs. Now, aren't these something? Holding them up to inspect them, I picture myself wearing them, then wince at the thought. With all these men on this ship, I dare not wear such a thing.

Digging deeper, I find a white dress with little blue flowers scattered throughout. It's perfect. It's made of lightweight cotton fabric and looks appropriate. Standing up, I hold it to myself. Now, this will work just fine. Shedding my heavy attire, I feel instant relief as I slip into the cooler gown.

Stepping out onto the deck, the lightweight dress makes all the difference. I walk to the rail, eager to let the breeze cool my body.

"It doesn't get any prettier than this," says Samuel as he passes by.

I smile at him. "It's ever-changing, isn't it? The water, that is."

"Yes, Miss. You never know from one minute to the next what color the sea's going to be. I've sailed to far-away places, been carried on great adventures, and seen many different things. That's why I sail. I find life on land too simple. My dad was a sailor and took me on a ship when I was just a young lad, and I've loved it ever since. Just give me water over land anytime."

"How deep do you think it is?"

"Ah, don't no one knows what's down there, but it's deep. Some say there's no bottom, and that there are monsters down there. But I don't let that bother me. I ain't never seen no monsters. You'll notice the water changing colors. Sometimes it's dark, the darkest blue you've ever seen, almost black; other times, it's as green as a frog, and then it can be light blue like a feather on a bluebird. She's always changing, kind of like you ladies. We men never know what color you're in. We just have to wait and test the waters." With that, he chuckles and walks on.

Smiling, I shake my head and laugh.

Suddenly, I hear a commotion of men yelling. What's going on? Running to the port side of the ship, I see one of the crewmen has his leg caught in a rope and is dangling high above. He looks to be unconscious. Is he dead?

I step back to stay out of everyone's way. Several men climb to the top of the mast, shimmying out on the main crossbeam, then slowly lower him to the deck.

Hearing men arguing, I go to where they're roughing up one of the crewman that's just come down from above. They drag him across the deck, then tie him to the ship's mast. Staying back, I want to see how the law on ship is carried out.

Captain Anthony is busy helping the men lower the unconscious man to the deck, then leans over him to see if he's still alive. I hear men saying that the two men got into an argument high up on the sail, and it resulted in one of them falling.

James comes over and stands beside me. "Do you know what happened?" I ask as I reach out and take his arm.

Looking at me with surprise, maybe because I took his arm, he tells me, "It isn't clear whether he was pushed or if he just lost his balance. If it hadn't been for his foot getting caught in a rope, he would have hit the deck and been killed."

The man's leg looks like it might be out of its socket. It seems to be dangling in an odd way. I didn't rush forward to help, nor have I told the crew that I worked at the hospital in prison. I hope James keeps his mouth shut. I'm not ready to step up to that kind of work again. Is that selfish of me? After all, the crewmen did rescue me. But I feel it best to stay away from the men as much as possible.

Captain Anthony walks over to the man who's tied to the mast, grabbing him by his shirt. "George, what the hell happened?" he demands.

"I don't know. Me and Denis, we're just talking and down he goes."

"That's not what I hear. Some heard and saw the two of you arguing up there."

"No, captain, we were just discussing something, and down he went," he answers again.

"Take him below and put him in irons till I find out what happened!" orders the captain.

"Wait, I'll tell you. He wouldn't shut his 'ole. He says disrespectful things about the lady." Looking sheepishly at me, George continues, "He told me what he wanted to do to her. That's when I told 'im to shut his arse 'ole, and I swung to smack 'im. I didn't know he wasn't 'oldin' on. For sure, I didn't mean to make 'im fall. 'Tis true, Captain, I didn't like him talkin' about the lady like that."

The captain nods. "Mr. Smith."

"Captain?"

"Have George taken below."

"Aye, Captain."

Then the captain goes to the unconscious man. Looking at Peat, he tells him, "Take Denis and fix him. Now, all you men get back to work. There's a ship to sail!" The captain walks away, glancing over at me with uncertainty.

That afternoon they bring George back up on deck and tie him to the mast. I cringe when I see what's about to happen. He's to be lashed. He broke one of the strict rules of the ship. No fighting while aloft. It has to be done. No matter if the man was in the right or not, he broke the rule and has to suffer the punishment.

Panicking, I can't watch. Horrible memories of being whipped at the prison flood over me. As I hear the crack of the whip and screams of pain that follow, I cup my hands over my ears and run below.

Hurrying down the stairs I step on my dress, ripping it, and nearly tumble. Looking for a place to hide, I go to my bed on the floor. Muffling my scream in my blankets, I cry.

What is this curse of mine?

28

It's been days since Denis fell from the mast. He's now able to come up on deck with a brace under his arm so he can walk, but he won't be much help. He stands on deck most of the day looking up. It's apparent he wants to be with the others. George, on the other hand, is high above seeing about his duties. They must have settled their differences because I see Denis waving at him. How strange it is, they nearly kill each other, then forget all about it and go back as if nothing's happened.

The bell rings, signaling an approaching storm. Captain Anthony tells us this one appears to be massive and will be upon us soon.

With dark clouds above, our ship starts to groan from the force of the wind and waves. Soon water crashes across the deck, tossing us like a helpless piece of drifting wood. I'm getting used to the storms but still wonder how our ship can stay together through all this. The roar of howling wind sounds angry, like screams calling to take us under. Maybe I've become somewhat crazy, but still, there's a beauty and excitement, even in the danger of it all. The waves break over the deck like giant hands ready to pull us down into the deep. The crew hurries to secure the sails while listening to the captain's orders, then yell back their needs.

The rain is starting to blow sideways as the ship pitches, making it difficult for the men high up on the mast. I've seen these men in action. They are strong, skilled, and know how to do their jobs. Fearlessly, they climb the mast, maneuvering across the riggings out to the rain-soaked sails. These men are unafraid of the sea. Their passion for adventure thrills them as they journey these deep waters. They've had this battle many times and know exactly what they need to do.

I stand in gratitude and awe, watching these men who love the challenge of the sea. They put their lives in danger on these waters to make sure we are safe.

This storm is different, they say. It's a deadly monster that could smash our ship to pieces. Samuel says it's probably a hurricane, and the captain will try to go around it, but it's going to be rough.

Water seeps through the planks and timbers where the pitch has worn away. The crew hurries to tightly batten down everything while rats scurry up the stairs as the saltwater begins to flood the floor of the cargo hold. Do you know how many places there are on this ship where water can seep through? And rat! I've seen more than I want to count.

Crouching against a wall, I try to stay out of everyone's way. I see James helping secure ropes that keep the sails in place.

All the lanterns have been extinguished for fear of fire, which makes being below pitch black. With no light and the ship rocking, there's always danger of being crushed by the heavy cargo that can break loose. I like the dark, but not that kind of dark, so I stay above, trying to be brave despite huge waves crashing across the deck. I know I should go to the hatch, but I'm afraid to let go. So I stay where I am.

Ropes start coming loose from the riggings as giant pulleys swing past, making it even more dangerous. I cower in a small corner near the bridge.

I hear the crew yelling at each other, trying to secure the lines to keep the ship safe. James and the others are busy helping too. When there's a need they fit right in, working together.

More rats come from below and thankfully wash overboard. Where have they all come from? And to think, I've been sleeping on the floor.

Holding tightly to the railing by the steps leading up to the quarterdeck, I worry, will this storm ever end? Suddenly, the ship rolls almost completely on its side as the giant masts drag through a massive wave. I can hear timbers cracking as the roar of the sea batters our ship.

Screaming, I use both hands to hold on as I start to slide across the deck towards the sea. Wrapping both arms around the rail, I pray it won't snap. Struggling to hold tight, I watch as one of the crew is swept overboard and pulled under by an angry wave. Horrified, I scream with terror, burying my face in my arms.

Did I come on this escape only to die at sea? Thoughts of the prison flood over me. What if I hadn't chosen to kill my father? Who would I be now? Might I have found happiness? Would I have children? So much of my life is my fault.

Suddenly the salty seawater splashes in my face, bringing me back to the present danger. Taking hold of the moment to find my courage, I tighten my grip and pray. Please, God, help me.

One of the crew sees me huddling in the corner and makes his way over to me. "Come with me, Miss," he yells over the wind, reaching out his hand.

It's Jackson. My hand grips his as he takes hold of mine. Making our way to the hatch, I yell, "No! It's too dangerous down there!"

"Trust me," he shouts over the wind.

Then, I let him lead me below.

In the darkness I cling to him as he feels his way to a narrow opening. "This is where we keep the extra ropes," he yells over the noise. "Crawl in here, and you'll be safe."

Trusting him, I climb in. It's pitch black and smells like rope and the captain's stinky wet dog. No telling how many rats are in here too. It might reek, but it's dry, and I do feel safer. Then Jackson's gone.

Alone, I stay in the dark curled up in a ball like a frightened child. Feeling the ship pitching violently, all I can do is stay here and listen to the high-pitched tones blowing through the riggings and the roar of the sea as the ship groans from the strain.

From exhaustion, I must have fallen asleep. When I awake, a little sunlight is coming in through one of the portholes which must have come open during the storm. The ship is calmer now, not pitching violently any longer. It's finally over.

I crawl out of my space and make my way up top. The danger has passed, and now it's just the ordinary winds blowing. I look up and see the sails hoisted high and open to the breezes, as they should be. Our ship has won the battle and is cutting through the waves again.

The men's faces are grim on deck, however. They say two of the crewmen are missing. I quietly tell them I saw Brady swept overboard. No one knows what's happened to the other missing man. The reality of loss sets in, and I can see it on their faces. The captain and crew stay busy assessing the ship's damages, but I see their sadness.

Climbing down the steps, I go below to see if I can help Peat in the galley. I might as well make myself useful. If I could cook at the prison, I can help cook on the ship.

The saltwater has damaged most of the dry goods stored below. The flour is wet, so we have to use it before it spoils.

The ship meals never were nutritious nor attractive, but now they're going to get even worse. Poor Peat has a particularly thankless job. Many of the men mutter at what he fixes, but I'm grateful and understand it's hard.

Walking up on deck to toss trash overboard, I see the destruction from the massive storm. There's nothing left of the fresh food that had been stored on deck. The cages that held the chickens and rabbits have been smashed, and all washed overboard during the storm. They found the goat still attached to its rope, but it had drowned from the massive waves that engulfed the ship. My heart sinks as I watch the men cut it loose, then take it below to be cooked.

Some of the crew go to secure the provisions and cargo that broke free, and that's when they find the other missing crewman. The loose cargo must have crushed him when it shifted. No one knew he had gone below, so it was sometime before they found him. By then, the rats had already started feeding on him. It must have been a gruesome sight for them.

I'm amazed at how quickly they wrap his body for burial. It's unsafe to keep anything dead on board for fear of disease, so overboard he must go.

Everyone gathers on deck as Captain Anthony commends the man's body to the deep. It's sad to see the shipmates gather around the oblong wrapped canvas containing his remains. As the body slides down the plank and into the sea, I hear eight bells, which means end of watch. Captain speaks a few words about the two lost men that bring little comfort. Everyone gazes off the back as the ship moves through the water, leaving the rippling wake behind. The canvas-covered body floats for a moment as if to say goodbye, then disappears beneath the sea. I look at the crew and how their faces tell their stories. Silent tears roll down their cheeks. They know this is life and death on this vast ocean, but still they sail.

⁂

"Give that back to me, you scruffy dog!" I yell while reaching for the scrub brush. Determined, I chase the dog across the deck while trying to get the brush back from him.

"You thief, I'll just have to throw you overboard if you don't let me give you a bath. You stink!"

It takes me a good while to corner Scraps, but he's all mine now. Wrapping a rope around his neck, I drag him to the pail as his four legs stiffen in defiance. Securing the rope to the mast, I make sure he won't get away.

"All right, you can keep the brush in your mouth. Maybe that will keep you from biting me."

Pulling away, he growls at me with the brush still in his mouth. But it's no use, and I soon have him covered in a soapy lather.

"Poor dog," says one of the crew.

"I wouldn't mind if she wants to give me a bath," says another.

I hear the crew chucking, and they make me smile.

"He's never had a bath!" one yells to me.

"Well, he's getting one now!" I yell back. "He smells!"

I hear James laughing with the others as they watch me wrestle the unruly dog. Scraps looks humiliated as he drops his soapy head while still holding the brush with a firm bite. But he doesn't have a choice; he isn't getting out of it.

"I promise you'll be happier when I get through with you. Now, hold still!" I tell him.

"I must say, Miss Adeleen, I didn't think it could be done," Captain says.

"Anything can be done. You just need to do it," I tell him.

Captain Anthony takes a long look at me, then looks down at the pitiful sight of his dog. He grins and nods before turning and walking away.

"There! You're all done. Now maybe I might like you," I say as I untie the rope. With a dash, Scraps is gone.

Shaking and bouncing across the deck, he's liking the new feeling of being clean. Then he stops to play. Dropping the brush at my feet, he then jumps back.

I giggle. "Well, do I have a new friend now?"

⁂

The crew's starting to get restless again. With nothing to do, tensions among the men are building. Again some loudly voice their dislikes at having us on the ship.

"Ring the bell, Mr. Smith. I want all hands on deck immediately. It seems that I need to give them a talking to," says the captain.

"Aye, Captain," Samuel says as he reaches up to ring the bell. "All hands on deck! Captain's got something to say, so you'd better listen."

Standing before his crew, Captain Anthony begins. "Yes, we have a woman on board," he firmly reminds them, as if they need it pointed out.

"She don't belong here," grumbles one of the men.

"Well, she is, and you're just going to have to deal with it. I don't want to hear any more grumbling out of you men," he orders.

"She's trouble," yells another.

"Yes, well, so am I," says the captain. "If any of you want to find out, you try. Now, I want you to treat her like a lady and respect her. That means stop the harassing words and glares. You'll be back home soon enough, and you can find all the women you want. Just you never mind her.

"Yea, he just wants her for himself," one mutters, as others laugh.

"I'll have any man in irons if needs be," says the captain.

"Captain, she's the reason we've had the bad luck. It's her fault those two men are dead," say one of the crew.

"If you believe that, Andrews, then you're a fool," replies the captain. "Now, back to work. We have a long way to go, and this ship needs all of you to sail her."

A few of the men pass by me giving a sheepish nod, which I think is their way of saying, "We're glad you're on board." Still others glare at me, making it obvious they aren't going to listen to the captain. Worried, I don't know what to do.

We've been at sea for nearly two months, and Samuel says the last storm has blown us far off course, so now it's a guess where we might be. There's no moon and thick clouds cover the stars, so it must be difficult for our captain to navigate. Samuel says the captain can only rely on his compass at this point, so it requires all the more skill. With most of the sails damaged during the last storm, our ship is moving slow against the currents.

As day goes into darkness, a watchman walks the deck carrying a dimly lit lantern, while Scraps follows closely behind, probably thinking he'll get fed. With the food supply dwindling, I'm sure there's not much left for the dog. Not that the dog needs extra food.

How peacefully the winds blow across the calm waves. A light fog starts to roll in, but most likely will be gone by morning. And so it is as we sail towards America.

❦❦❦❦❦

Waking early, I climb the stairs just as the morning sun begins to bathe the sky, bringing on a glow. Going to my favorite place just below the quarterdeck, I watch the sunrise. Someone has put a heavy wooden chair on the deck just for me. From there I can sit as we travel north.

It gets tiring watching the water all the time, but there's not much to do while on board. I find myself looking at the waves without seeing them, lost in my thoughts. It helps me to think while I figure out my life. I try to imagine what I will do first when I get to America.

Soon James walks over and plops down on the deck next to me. Mornings have been our time to talk about so many things. Maybe this is a good time for my confession.

"James, there's something I've been wanting to tell you. Something I've been keeping from you, and I want you to know."

Looking at me with curiosity, he says, "Sounds serious, what is it?"

"Well, you know when you and the men gave me those notes for the prison break?"

"Yes, what about 'em?" he asks.

"Well...I can't read."

"What? You...? Then how did you?" he stops himself, not believing me.

"No, you have to listen to me. I know I should have told you then, but I was afraid if I did, you'd think you wouldn't need me. So, I kept quiet. I never showed another living soul those notes," I reassured him.

James throws his head back and laughs.

Striking him on his shoulder, I look at him, "What's so funny?"

"No, no, you did well, Adeleen. We never knew. You are a sly one, aren't you," smiling.

"No, just desperate," I reply. "I wanted to get out of that prison any way I could, so I lied."

Putting one arm around me, he gives me a quick squeeze. "I'm glad you did lie, that way I get to keep you," he replies.

What? What does he mean? Looking at him, I don't know what to say. This scares me.

29

It's been so long since we've had anything fresh to eat. The storm made sure of that when it washed our chickens overboard and ruined our supplies. It didn't take long for the goat meat to be eaten. Even catching fish is a challenge. The ocean waters are getting warmer as we move north, which means there should be more fish, if we can catch them. The men keep a line and hook over the side, always hoping one might bite.

Fish!

I don't think it's a whale, but it sure is a big fish, the biggest I've ever seen. My nails rip into it as I help to bring it onboard. Others grab it, making sure this one isn't going to flip away. Everyone shouts cheers as the giant blue fish flips around on deck. Its scales glistens silver and blue in the sunlight.

"Good eatin' tonight," someone shouts.

"Aye, it's a big one," I say in wonderment.

Slowly the men hoist it high up by its tail so they can clean out its guts. I jump back as they split open its belly and the innards fall. It doesn't bother me — I've seen worse while working in the prison hospital. I've seen men's innards hanging out after they had been in a fight, but I shake my head to remove the memory.

Enjoying the fun, I stand back and see how catching this large fish has made everyone feel happier. Even Scraps feels the excitement as his tail wags happily while he eats what's dropped on the deck.

A few of the men stand beside the giant fish, putting their hand to the top of their head, as to measure themselves to it. I too take my turn standing beside it. Looking up, I think I'd better never fall in the water because a fish like this might easily swallow me whole.

"How do we cook such a big fish?" I ask.

"Hell, I'll eat it raw," says one.

"Cook knows how," says the captain. "Good work," he says as he slaps the shoulder of the man who caught it. "Now, let's get back to sailing!"

❧❧❧❧❧❧

I look for something to keep me busy, and someone tells me I can help repair the sails if I'd like. The sails are always in need of mending. There is plenty to sew, and I want to work.

Preacher Man Haley is in charge of the mending and shows me how important it is to stitch the sails a certain way to make the torn spots strong again. I don't mind sewing. I'm certainly not strong enough to climb high on the mast, nor do I want to. I'll leave that job to the men.

"Are you a real preacher?" I ask him.

"No, they just call me that 'cause I trust in God," he says. "Whenever something bad happens, I'm always praying, calling out to God."

"Does he hear you?" I ask.

"I'd like to think he does," he says, smiling.

"I've done a lot of bad things in my life I'm sorry for."

"He forgives you, if you truly are."

Looking at him, I wonder... *Can God really forgive me?*

"I have God's Book, but I can't read so good," he says.

"I can relate to that," I tell him. "I can't read either. I went to school when I was little, but when things happened and I went away, I never got to learn again, and I've forgotten almost all of it. I had no mind to read in prison."

"Maybe someday I'll learn to read proper. Some of those words in my book are mighty big," he says, laughing. "All I know is, I've seen many a man dying, or thinking they were going to die, and call out to God. I'd like to know where that comes from. Some of them don't even believe in Him. But when something bad happens, they start calling to God for help. It's a real mystery to me."

"You're right. I remember when I've called out to God plenty of times, but He didn't answer, and I didn't see Him. Back in Australia, I even got to go into His house one time and got to see where He sits, but He wasn't there."

"He wasn't?" he replies.

Smiling, I tell him, "Someday, I'd like to see that book of yours."

He nods as we continue mending the much-needed sails.

While sitting comfortably on deck repairing the canvas, two of my Irishmen walk up. I say 'my,' because we came from hell to freedom together.

I look up, and both Darragh and Michael are standing shirtless before me. They're holding out their shirts before them, with big grins on their faces.

"Hey, Adeleen," says Michael. "We both have rips in our shirts and ask if you might stitch them up for us?"

"Aye," says Darragh.

I laugh at both of them. These rugged Irishmen are pretending to be helpless.

Then, with a shock that sends a tremor through me, I notice a "D" burned into Michael's chest, just like the one on James'. I try not to stare. Although I want to ask, I don't. It floods my memories with images of the prison again, but I shake them away.

"What did you do to these?" I ask, taking one of the ripped shirts and holding it up.

Both of them look at each other and smile.

"Just no-good shirts from hell."

"You want me to toss them overboard?" I ask, and start to ball them up.

"No…don't throw them away. They are all we have to wear. We weren't given a trunk of clothes when we came on board, so we guess you might mend them for us," Michael says, smirking.

"All right, you two, take your half-naked bodies away so they won't distract me," I say as I snicker back.

"Oh, yes, Ma'am," Darragh says as they both bow, covering their chests and backing away.

❧❧❧❧❧

Being a woman and going through my female time is not easy on a ship with all men. Even though they try to give me space to sleep, there's very little privacy.

I get creative and steal some cloth from the galley, only to hear Cook yelling, "Where are all my rags?" I keep an innocent look on my face when he complains. It's all I can do since I don't want to announce it. Of course, I can't wash them. Where would I hang them to dry? So, I pitch them overboard.

Thinking back to the first time I experienced my blood, I was twelve. I remember it was on the transport ship that was taking me to Australia. Little did I know this happens to a young girl as she grows into a woman, but I soon learned. Since I lost my mum at a young age, she hadn't prepared me for what was to happen when I got older.

Twice a day on the prison ship, and a guard would come below to give everyone a drink of water. It was difficult for us prisoners because the guards would go by us so fast. Sometimes I wouldn't get to drink, but I soon learned to get myself up on my knees to make sure I was ready when they came past. If anyone stayed sitting, the guards wouldn't make an effort, so the prisoner would go without.

After my drink, I would sit back to rest against the ship's side. I recall I didn't feel very well, and my insides hurt. As I looked down I saw blood, lots of it, running down my legs, I gasped and started to scream while trying to stand to see what was happening. One of the older women close by me grabbed my arm and pulled me back down, then told me to shut up. I looked at her with wide eyes.

"I'm dying," I told her in terror, as I tried wiping it off.

"No, you're not. It will go away in a few days. Now, shush," she whispered. "The guards will hear you."

I shook my head. "I don't understand."

"You will later. Now just shut yer mouth."

I was confused and scared. How does she know I'm not dying? I sat down and glared at her. Then she pulled up her skirt, and I saw dried blood on the inside of both her legs. I looked back down at my legs and began to cry. I am dying. She doesn't know what she's talking about. Mine is worse than hers, and she's dying too, I thought. Crying, I felt hopeless. Just wait, I know I'm right. I closed my eyes and fell asleep, knowing for sure that I'd be gone in the morning.

Such innocence.

❦❦❦❦❦❦

The long trip weighs heavy on us all, and boredom is still the constant problem. Many of the crew gamble, which brings about fights from a poor loser. Someone is always playing music. A few have carved wooden flutes, while others have brought their string fiddles and other strange instruments with them.

The captain has put a limit on everyone's drinking rum for now. When there's plenty to do, then it will flow more freely again.

The Irish six have their share of drinking, especially James. He's always downing the rum, more than the other five, and he isn't good at holding it either, which means he's trouble. If he's had too much to drink, he wants to pick an argument with someone. It isn't a good thing. The other five will often step in and pull him away, trying to stop a fight.

Being around the men isn't exactly pleasant for me, especially if they're drunk. There's constant profanity as they curse and swear. Although I'm not much better, I still don't always feel safe. There are several men who I have to be careful around. I've seen them talking and looking at me. It's the same way the guards at the prison would watch me. But I still keep my old rusty knife hidden in my clothing. No swine of a man is ever going to rape me again.

My heightened awareness of danger resurfaces when I see the stares, and feel something terrible is going to happen.

I have hopes and dreams for America, so I wish this ship would hurry and get there. I know I'll be happy there. I know it.

Below deck, while I make my way back from relieving myself, one of the crew steps out, blocking me from going forward. I stand frozen for the moment. As I go to move past, he reaches out and grabs me, pinning me against the cargo. Then another sailor comes from behind him. I let out a scream as the first one quickly puts his hand over my mouth, trying to muffle me. I bite him, and he pulls his hand away. Pulling my knife from my dress pocket, I point the sharp point to his belly. What a surprised look on his face when he feels the sharp blade. Quickly, he releases his hold on me, throwing his hands in the air as if to say he understands. I don't think he'd known how dangerous I can be.

Seeing what I did scares the hell out of the second man and he's gone. This one stands frozen in front of me with the point of my knife ready to slit him open. Some of the Irishmen hear my screams and come running down the steps. Seeing the sailor standing in front of me, James grabs him, pulling him back. I step away and quickly hide my knife.

"I'm all right. I slipped, and he caught me."

The man who grabbed me looks at me in disbelief, then quickly goes up on deck. With all the commotion, others have come below to see what's happening, including the captain. He asks what's going on. I tell him everything is fine, no trouble.

I look around, but neither man is anywhere close. I'm sure they're lying low. After that, I hope the word gets out to the crew that I carry a knife and they should think hard whether it's worth a split gut or not.

I soon realize that if this keeps up the captain will have the whole crew in irons.

✻✻✻✻✻✻

The relenting heat makes it hard to breathe. The fact that we are on water makes it all the worse. The damn humidity causes my every breath to weigh me down. The sweltering sun bakes down on us and the wind has died. We're at the equator, and our ship is becalmed. It's like Samuel told me, "It's hellish hot."

166

There are no waves today. The water swells, almost like it's alive and breathing. So we stay stalled, bobbing on the glassy sea, waiting for the wind.

Tonight everyone sleeps on the deck, hoping to find a hint of a slight breeze. With starry nights above and the moon glistening on the water, our ship lies motionless and will continue that way for twelve more days.

The crew lowers buckets into the sea to gather water so we can drench ourselves. We do whatever we can to get relief and stay cool. I wish I could swim. I might even jump in the water like some of the men are doing. They aren't afraid of sharks or monsters below.

"Ah, this ain't nothing. I'd seen it so devilish hot the pitch between the boards of the ship melted," one of the crew tells me.

"Yea, then you'd better look for the leaks. These here ships, they sure can leak," says another.

My eyes widen with the thought of the ship leaking. If all the pitch melts, what will hold it together?

The crew can see they frightened me by my expression, and begin to laugh.

"Oh, you're just joshing me," I say feeling foolish.

I look over at James, and he just smiles and shrugs.

"No, we ain't, Miss," says another sailor.

I can tell they enjoy frightening me, but is it true?

Under the stars is the place to sleep on these hot nights. I walk across, stepping over others that are laid out across deck, all the while inspecting the pitch between the boards.

❧❧❧❧❧

I'm captivated by how giant the sails are and how they capture the wind when it blows. There's a slight breeze today but not enough to push us anywhere. The days seem longer than ever, and tempers are growing short, including mine. I would give anything to feel a cool breeze touch the drops of sweat on my body, yet the weather stays hot and sticky.

The men are getting louder and continue to be restless. They're getting into scuffles, knocking things over, and occasionally the captain intervenes, but mostly not. I see they have respect for him, and some even fear him. They've heard stories about him, but they aren't sure if those stories are fact or fiction. I'm sure they don't want to find out. No one wants to tell me the stories, so I don't ask.

I can sense the tension. When we first came on board, the six Fenians kept pretty much to themselves, away from the crew, but now they intermingle more. Brawls aren't uncommon now. How can you have all these men on a ship and not get on each other's nerves? Hell! They get on my nerves. I wouldn't mind punching a few.

I see Darragh and Hassett looking at the crew and laughing, almost taunting them, which doesn't sit well. When I walk over to speak to James, one of the crewmen bumps me, nearly knocking me down. Oh no, that's all it takes. James grabs him and swings, landing his fist on the man's ear. Then, it's an all-out fight between the two.

We all gather around, and then before I know it, everyone, and I mean everyone, is fighting! Someone grabs me, so I turn and swing and hit them in the face, only to find out it's the captain trying to pull me out of the way.

"Oh, I'm sorry. Did I hurt you?"

Touching his hand to his lip, he laughs, then says, "They're just blowing off steam. I'll let them fight this time, so it's best if you stay back."

"What if they hurt each other?" I ask.

"They probably will, but as long as no one goes overboard, then I'll let them have at it. These men need this," he tells me.

The captain is right. Before long, there are bloody men sprawled out everywhere across the deck. Those who need more attention find themselves down in the galley for Peat to stitch. I see James looking pretty beat up but still standing. By the way, where was Peat when all this is happening? I didn't see him up here fighting. I chuckle, thinking, he was probably waiting below with his needle and thread.

After it's all over and the men have fought to near exhaustion, they're right back sitting and laughing together. Amazing!

The crew are somewhat a bunch of misfits, because they don't seem to fit together. They are all different and from different places in the world. Samuel tells me that some of the original crew quit at the last port before they got to Australia. He says it's not uncommon for a ship to lose some of their crew at every port. That's how men travel to see the world. So, the captain has to pick up what crew he can before going on.

30

I've tried to learn their names, but there are too many, and not everyone wants to talk to me. Samuel says each man has a story to tell. Some of the men seek adventure, and some are probably running from something — could be the law. Looking at them, I'm still not quite sure if I can trust any of them.

Intently watching the endless horizon as the sun gets closer to touching the water, I'm unaware of my immediate surroundings when suddenly a voice startles me.

"What do you see?"

It's Captain Anthony stepping down from the quarterdeck and approaching me. His dark curls, peeking out from under his hat, are teased by the gentle breeze. I find myself staring at him for just a moment, then looking away.

"Water. Lots and lots of water. How much longer until we to get to America?" I ask gazing at the water.

"A few more months, but it won't be without adventure and danger," he tells me as he walks closer.

"What's it like in America?"

"It's what you want it to be. It's a young country," he tells me, moving even closer.

Looking at him, I'm taken by how handsome he is. "I've never been anywhere except England and the Australian prison. Do you think it will be easier there?"

"What do you mean easier?" searching my eyes with a slight questioning look.

"In England, life for many was a hardship. I know I was very young, but I still remember people struggling. And then at the prison, it was just downright hell." I look up to the sky then continue. "I guess I want to know what it's like to be free and to have a real life. I don't want to do any of those things I had to do in prison to survive. Do you think it will be better there?"

By the look on his face, he probably doesn't know what to say with all my babbling. How can he? He knows nothing about what I've been through, or what I had to do to survive. Without answering, he reaches out his hand, and I take it, putting my arm through his as we slowly begin to walk the deck.

"God has a plan for you, Adeleen, and you just have to let him show you."

Looking to the sky's soft clouds I ask myself. *Where is God?*

The bell rings, and it's time to eat, but I find myself not wanting to end my time with the captain.

"Will you dine with me and the others this evening? No telling what Cook's come up with, but I'd like you to join us," he adds while putting out his hand, escorting me to the door leading to his dining quarters.

"Thank you, yes. I think I'd like that," I answer while looking around, hoping James isn't watching.

I feel so honored to be invited to dinner with him, Mr. Smith, Mr. Breslin, and Mr. Desmond.

Standing, they nod at me as I enter the room. Nodding back, I'm shown an empty chair beside the captain. I see Christian standing dutifully ready to serve as the captain motions for the food to be brought.

I've had very little interaction with Mr. Breslin, and none whatsoever with Mr. Desmond, although I've seen him on upper deck. I know they came from America and were important in our escape, but I haven't been able to speak with them. These finely dressed men spend most of their time inside this grand dining room or on the quarterdeck away from others. Maybe they think they're better than everyone and don't want to associate with them. Kind of the way my father treated my mum. Other than what Samuel and Captain have told me, I don't know anything about these men.

With all eyes on me, Mr. Desmond is the first to speak. "First time sailing, Miss?"

"Not exactly, I was transported on a convict ship from England when I was just a young girl," I reply.

"Oh, I'm sorry. I didn't think. Forgive me," he stammers.

The captain quickly explains how the prisoners are treated while being chained aboard the transport ships. He doesn't get it right, polishing it a bit to make the men comfortable, but it sounds interesting to them. Gazing at me, I can tell they have questions. Even Mr. Smith looks away with embarrassment. They probably want to know what I did to be sent there, but I'm not offering that up unless one asks, and maybe not even then. I hope they're too gentlemanly to ask.

Breaking the silence, Mr. Smith starts telling some of his wild adventures while sailing. Soon we're all enjoying his stories, laughing and talking through dinner. I too begin to enjoy, although I don't know what the bloody hell I'm doing here, and feeling this is no place for me.

Finally getting up my nerve, I speak, "Tell me about this America."

"Well, picture this," Mr. Breslin says as he gladly lifts his hands as to paint a picture. "There are grand towns and land for those who want it, as far as the eye can see. They say there's a place for everyone, a place where you'll be able to build a home. America just came out of a Civil War, and now the Africans are free, no more slavery."

"Oh my," I say, thinking of Rou.

"There's a government that gives everyone freedom to dream and grow. You'll like it there," adds Mr. Desmond proudly.

It's nice to hear. I now have a feeling of safety with the dreams of my new home, and don't ever want it to change. All the anger and hurt within me is beginning to be replaced with hope as I hear more about America.

After we've had our fill, Captain Anthony invites me to walk on deck. I take his arm as we pass through the door out into the fresh night air. How quiet and peaceful it is on the ship. Everyone, except the deck watchman and the man high up in the crosstree, has gone below to drink and gamble, which is where James probably is.

It is a magical moment for me. We both look over at the men. And they're watching all right, one with a big toothy smile. The captain gives a quick motion of his head to the man on deck and then raises his hand, signaling for the man up high to look elsewhere.

Unable to move and not wanting this moment to end, I stand with the captain in the moonlight. My heart beats faster as he slowly puts his hand around my waist and draws me close. Leaning in, he kisses me. I have no power to resist, so I linger, as my whole being feels his closeness. Unsure how I should act, I hesitate. I feel my face flush and wonder, shy? Why am I shy? This isn't me; shyness has never happened to me before. But never has such a man been so gentle with me. My mind begins to swim as I feel him close.

Then he whispers in my ear, "Come to my cabin with me."

I take a long look at him, studying his face and eyes. Is this what I want? Hell yes, it is, but I don't know, as my mind is full of confusion. He has given me so much, is he expecting it?

"I don't think I should, sir," I answer.

Trying to find myself, I question my actions. If I sleep with every man who wants me, or I want, what will I be? With that, I take a step back and bid him goodnight.

Am I becoming a lady? Maybe, and I like it.

⁂

We've been at sea for months now, and today the wind gusts are light with very little movement. There's no sign of any storm clouds that might be heading our way. Every day on the ship is different, bringing new challenges, and new adventures. The riggings hang quietly again, since the sails are only half full of wind. A man climbs high above, and one climbs down for change of shift. They've told me there's a fear more canvases might have been ripped from the last storm, so this is a good time to inspect them. Such care is taken with this ship. Every tension must be right for the sails that are waiting for the much-needed wind.

We are in great need of food. I, like the others, am starting to feel the effects of hunger. Fresh water was captured from the last rainstorm, but supplies are dwindling. Captain Anthony orders half rations until we can find land.

There's something about this endless voyage. Hopefully, high winds, when they come, will blow us in the direction we need to go. Please, I plead silently, just push us towards some land.

The ship moves ever so slowly with each gust, while everyone keeps an eye out for land. The water is calm as if we were on a giant lake. Not a ripple on it, just a glassy calm. I help watch the horizon but see nothing except the vast sea. Our ship bobs on the water, but even that little motion is starting to bother me more than usual. It is not like when I first got on ship. Back then, I heaved my guts out.

This time it's different and I'm feeling weak. I'm sure it's from the lack of fresh food. All that's left to eat is the salt pork, and that's not good. There's a real danger of scurvy. I taste blood in my mouth as my gums are starting to bleed.

Maybe if I just lie down on the deck, I'll feel better. Finding my favorite spot beside my big chair I drop myself to the deck and curl up, where James and the others are sprawled out. I can't help but wonder, will we ever make it?

My hopes of traveling safely across this vast ocean overwhelm me. Is it all worth the risk? I look up, and my hope returns. Something is flying overhead. Well above the sails, it soars. I get up and see the water has turned to a beautiful light blue, not that dark blue from the deep that I've seen for so long. This must be the changing colors that Samuel had told me would happen.

Looking to the sky I see birds. "Hey!" I scream and point at them. "Look!"

"Land ahoy!" cries the man high up on the mast's crosstree.

Excited, I look up to him to see the direction he's pointing. The others race to the railing with me to see.

"Land ahoy!" the lookout shouts again.

Squinting to see better, I scan the horizon where the water meets the sky. Yep, there it is — a small dark speck well in the distance. With renewed hope and a spark of strength, my desire for life soars with that bird. Land, beautiful land rising from the ocean. I can't take my eyes from it. How long will it take to get there? Are there any people living there? Will there be food? I have so many questions, and like a child, my excitement grows.

Captain Anthony is busy with First Mate Samuel looking at maps and charts. They're trying to figure out what island it might be, and how far the ship's been blown off course.

Excitedly, some of the crew climb up the masts so they can get a better glimpse. It's a welcoming sight for us all. I know it is for me.

The current is helping take us closer, but still, it isn't enough. If only there were more wind. I see the island in the distance, but it doesn't seem to get any bigger. I watch Captain Anthony look through his spyglass, sweeping across the land. He and Samuel are pointing and talking. I'm sure they're deciding, with such little wind, how to get us there. I can feel my heart pounding with excitement. Hurry up, ship. Start moving!

James comes over to stand by my side and says just what I was thinking. "How are we ever going to get there?"

"I know. It's so far away."

"Make the boats ready!" yells the captain. "I need every oarsman."

"Aye, Captain!

"Lower all the boats!" yells Mr. Smith.

I look back towards the land. It's so far for the men to row. Then I remembered how far they rowed during our prison break. They rowed day and night non-stop.

The men lower the four whaleboats into the water and climb in. What they do next amazes me. Rowing in front of the ship, they're thrown ropes.

"Those crazy men are going to try and pull this ship," says James.

One oarsman stands and yells out a rhythm for all to hear…"PULL! PULL! PULL!"

Nothing.

Suddenly, I hear the ropes stretching under the enormous weight of the ship. How will they ever do such a thing, and what makes them think they can?

Then, ever so slowly, the ship begins to move. I watch from the front of the ship, taken in by this mastery.

I hear the crew's laughter as the ship slowly begins to move through the water. One of the men yells up to me, "Hey, Adeleen. I wager you didn't think we could do it, did you?"

I smile and wave while quietly thinking about these unbelievable men who can probably do anything once they set their minds to it.

Our giant ship moves forward ever so slowly, gliding with utter ease and smoothness across the glassy water. After rowing for what seems like hours, I suddenly feel the ship lunge. Looking up, I see the sails fill with wind.

The men cheer as they drop the ropes and quickly row back to the ship. Laughing and full of pride, they climb on board, then hoist their whaleboats back onto the ship and secure them safely.

Standing on deck with James and others, I watch as we sail towards the land. Amazed at what I have just seen, I enjoy the crew's triumph and excitement.

Pointing to the water, Samuel tells us the captain will be careful not to take the ship too close to the island for fear there might be reefs. They can rip the bottom right out of our ship if he's not careful.

Captain Anthony orders his men to keep an eye out for any life that might be on the island. Eagerly, I stand at the rail and help them look. Young Christian tells James and me that it appears to be a small island, so the chance of people living there is slim. Morry is busy dropping a weighted rope into the water, then brings it back up again, calling out numbers that tells the captain the water depth.

Soon orders are given. "Mr. Smith, house the mast! And, tell Mr. Stuart 'single anchor'!"

"Aye, Captain!"

Samuel shouts out orders for the crew to secure the sails as the ship becomes a flurry of activity. "Mr. Stuart, you heard your captain. Drop single anchor."

"Aye!" yells Mr. Stuart.

The heavy chain lowers the giant anchor, splashing it into the water, taking hold and slowing us to a stop.

"Three boats, Mr. Smith. We're going ashore."

"Aye, Captain!"

As they lower the boats, I wish I could go, but know better. Captain Anthony and his crew, armed with weapons, climb into the whaleboats eager to go ashore. Standing at the rails, I watch as the men row towards land. Reaching the beach, they climb out and scatter like ants moving up and down the shoreline, then disappear into the shrubs.

Eagerly waiting, I notice a sweet smell on the island breeze. Yes! There's got to be food there.

My fear mixes with excitement as I worry there might be hostile savages living on the island. Samuel once told me about some wild people who want to eat humans. My heart tightens as I think the men might be in danger. Suddenly, I hear a couple of shots coming from the shore.

"James," I say, tugging at the sleeve of his shirt. "Do you think they're all right?"

"I don't know," he answers, as we both stare at the shoreline.

31

The waiting is hard, and I get even more frightened as time goes on. I think to myself, this island must be dangerous.

"James, Samuel told me about savage people living on islands like this. Do you think they found them?"

"I can't say," says James.

Looking up to the helm, I see Samuel scanning the island with a spyglass. He hollers down and reassures us that everything will be all right.

That's what he thinks. I heard the shots, and they're not just shooting at rocks.

The day is almost gone and it will be dark soon, but still there's no sign of the men.

"Look!" says James pointing towards the shore.

The crew slowly emerges from the shrubs, carrying what hopefully is food. They load things onto the boats and then shove off back towards the ship. It's close to dark by the time the boats get back.

Yes! They've brought back a wild beast of some sort, and an abundance of fresh exotic fruit. What a welcome sight!

The men hoist the heavy animal aboard and then pull up the baskets of fruit. Jack, one of the crew, starts throwing fruit up onto the deck, so I run to help gather what I can while sinking my teeth into a sweet golden fruit.

"Make the ship secure for the night, Mr. Smith," says Captain Anthony. "We're staying for a few days. We'll send another crew ashore in the morning."

"Aye, Captain!"

"We're going to eat our fill tonight," says Captain Anthony with a handsome smile.

The next day the men are eager to take their turn going ashore with the captain. All four boats are let down. James and Michael climb into one, but I know I can't go, so I don't even ask. I'm just happy staying on deck, enjoying my very own freshly picked fruit.

Oh, the sheer joy! One of the crew comes over and asks me if he can sit down by me. "Sure," I say while enjoying my fruit with laughter. It's good to feel full again, I think. I hear him laugh at the way I relish my every bite. Well, what does he expect? Anything this delicious needs special care not to waste any. I take another juicy bite.

Breathing in the sweet, fresh, sea air, I lean back against the side of the ship. Sitting with a full stomach and feeling the sun warm me, my eyes get heavy and close. Suddenly, I feel his finger draw up my arm, caressing it. With that, I sit up, swinging, slapping the side of his head.

"Keep your sleazy hands off me, yer dogface scum!"

He sits back with such a start on his face. I don't think he knows what he's uncovered. I guess he's one who hasn't heard about my knife.

"Sorry, Miss," he says and hurries off.

The crew watching starts laughing. Glaring at them, I yell, "Go ahead and laugh. You try it and see how long you live." Old feelings come to the surface; feelings I wish were dead.

We stay anchored for two days while the men gather more food before we get under sail. Pulling up the anchor, we head north again. The ship begins to take to the wind as the men drop the three giant topsails. The sea changes daily as the storms blow in and out. With each one, I understand what to do to help and when to stay out of the way. I've gotten to like it when the squalls sometimes tower over the ship, rolling and pitching us like the giant piece of wood. My adventure is ever before me, and I have begun to enjoy even the dangers.

There's a steady wind blowing across the water again. It's hard to understand how there can be so much wind, and then it seems to blow away. Where does it go? The sea glistens with perfect rhythm as waves roll with a giant motion. Where does it all come from?

James walks over and sits beside me on deck. He reaches over and taps my shoulder, then gives me one of his pleasant smiles. Noticing sweat running down his bare chest, I look away, not wanting to stare. Well, I want to, but don't.

There's little wind, and the air is hot, but nothing near as hot as it was when we were at the equator. This is just the sweaty, tropical heat we're in right now. Fanning myself with a flat piece of wood, I ask, "How many days do you think it will be like this?"

"Only God knows," James answers. "I ask the same question too, and they tell me it might be a day, or even longer until the trade winds blow. We might becalm again.

"Be calm! What are you talking about? I'm done being calm. I thought all this stalling-out was over when we passed the equator." I say angrily.

James laughs, but I don't think it's funny.

"James, there's something I've been curious about, and I hope you don't mind me asking. You don't need to answer if you don't want. When I was treating you at the prison, I noticed a "D" burned into your chest, and I've seen the same on Michael's chest. Won't you tell me why they did that to you?"

"Aye, it ain't pretty is it?" he says. "Back in London when I was arrested, I was serving in the British military, but all along, me real loyalties were for Ireland. I guess you might say I was caught betwixt them loyalties. Before I knew it, they branded a 'D' in my chest for deserter. Michael was there at the same time and got the same treatment as me. Then they shipped us off to hell."

Resting my cheek on his arm, I hold him tight. "I'm sorry they did that to you. We all have scars, and some are just more visible than others."

"Aye."

"James, my thoughts are always racing to the newness of where we're going. I can't help but want to know how they live in America. How do they dress? What will the weather be like? What hardships will be there?"

"Aye, I've been wondering the same thing. It's going to be new, all right. A real gift for us all. We can start fresh and make a new life and finally put our ugly one behind. Aye…all new. Besides, it can't be too different. Don't forget, them Americans come from England."

Mopsy, one of the oarsmen, comes over to sit with James and me. He's always watching me and seems to have taking a liking for me, which makes me uncomfortable. James sees him hanging around me, and it doesn't sit well with him either.

"What was it like living in that place back in Australia?" he asks James and me.

"Hell," I answer, "Pure Hell!"

"I'm sorry," he says, "no lady as pretty as you should have been put there. What did you do that they had to send you there?"

I look at him and hesitate. Not wanting to answer, I look away. Will I ever be able to put my past behind me?

James answers for me, "Best to leave Hell in Hell,"

"Well, what was it? What did you do?" he asks a second time, pushing for an answer.

That's all it takes for James to take action. Grabbing the sailor by his shirt, and I'm sure some chest hairs, James lifts him to his feet and lays a good punch right in his face. The scuffle soon brings others who gather around.

As James and Mopsy hit each other, I wonder who is the stronger. I imagine the whaler is, but James is faster and keeps just out of his reach.

"Come on, James, hit him!" I shout.

It isn't pretty as blood starts to flow from both their noses. Then I realize I don't want them to fight after all, so I scream, "Stop!"

In seconds the crew gathers yelling for Mopsy, and the Fenians join in, cheering James.

What animals.

"Stop!" I scream again, but no one listens.

One of the crew tries to break them apart, but someone plants a fist in his face, and before I know it, they're all brawling again.

Is this something men have to do — almost kill each other?

I look up to the helm where the captain stands watching. Why isn't he stopping them? Is there going to be anyone left alive to sail the ship? Stupid men!

❧❧❧❧❧

Just then, the ship's bell starts ringing. Well, that stops everyone. But what does it mean?

"Thar she blows!" a voice yells as a man points to starboard.

It's amazing how the men stop fighting as the ship becomes a flurry of activity, and the crew's excitement heightens. They'd been waiting to hear these words that stir them. It's their chance to make chase and make the kill that puts money in their pockets.

The captain motions upward, and the tops sails drop from the wind, slowing the ship.

Looking towards the sun, the captain appears to wrestle with his decision. It only takes a moment of hesitation before he orders, "Stand down!"

I listen as some of the crew argue with him.

"We have plenty of time, Captain," pleads one of the men.

"Mr. Haley," the captain says firmly, "I say stand down."

The men have to let the whales swim away. It must be hard for them, not being able to chase these mammoth whales to their death. This is what they've been waiting for. This is why they signed on to this voyage.

The huge creatures roll gracefully through the water some distance from the ship. Some are blowing water high into the air and flipping their giant bodies as they surface from a deep dive. I stay along the rail, wanting to see more. The dog even enjoys the excitement and barks at the sight of the whales. Putting my hand over my brow to shade from the setting sunlight, I continue to watch them swim farther out to sea.

"Why aren't the men going after them?" I ask Samuel.

"There's little time to give chase. There's a greater danger after the sun goes down. The whaleboats and men could get lost in the dark."

The adventure in these men's hearts has taken a difficult turn. Some of them are angry to let the whales go, while others understand the captain's decision. They all know it, but still, some would risk their lives given the chance. These men will return to what they know, but that will have to wait for another time.

❦❦❦❦❦

The quarters below are stifling with thick smoke and curse words. The crew argues over the captain's decision. James and I sit listening to the men voicing their grievances. We both know that soon the men will put out their pipes and retire for bed, but until then, there'll be no peace.

"Come on, let's get some fresh air," says James, taking me by my hand.

I follow behind him as we step into the moonless night air. Wrapping my arm in his, I'm somewhat afraid. I don't like the deck when it's so dark, and rarely venture up when there's no moon.

Unable to see the water, I hear the waves lapping the side of the hull, and the gentle wind slapping the ropes against the mast. Except for the soft glow from the flickering light of the lantern hanging by the wheel on the quarterdeck, the night is eerie black.

James and I notice the watchman sitting on a crate fast asleep in a corner on the upper deck. When we chuckle, he suddenly sits up straight as if hoping we haven't seen him.

"It's a good thing there are no pirates out there that he needs to look out for," James says loudly.

I put my hand over my mouth to smother my giggle. "Shh, he'll hear you."

"Oh, that's all right, I'm sure it's not the first time he's gone to sleep on watch," says James a little louder so the other man can hear.

Together we hear the watchman chuckle, and we smile at him.

It feels good to laugh. My life is becoming more peaceful and happier, even though there's still a war of emotions that rage inside me. But for now, I'm grateful to be here. This trip is dangerous, that's

183

for sure. But I have learned my free life can be good, even when it's difficult.

"Listen," says James holding up his finger to his mouth for me to be still.

I try my best to listen but, what am I supposed to be listening for?

"Hear that? There it is again," he says.

"Yes, what is it?"

"It's the whales," says the watchman. "You can hear them blowing in the distance. You can even hear them singing to each other if you listen closely. If all is good, they'll still be here in the morning."

I hold my breath and stand still, listening for their incredible sounds.

"Listen! There they go again. Do you hear them, Adeleen?"

"Yes," I whisper. "I do. It's beautiful." I squeeze his arm.

I didn't know whales made noises like that. There's so much of life I want to learn.

James and I stay on deck for hours, watching the stars shoot across the moonless sky, and listening to the night sounds from the sea. I'm happy, happy to be by his side and free.

32

The next morning, I awaken to a ruckus up on deck. Quickly I climb the steps, eager to see what all the yelling's about. The whales must still be here. I run to the rail and see at least three giant whales spouting and flipping their tales in the distance.

The men look to the captain, waiting for instructions.

"Stand by to lower!" orders the captain.

"Three boats, Mr. Smith."

"Aye, Captain."

The men cheer with excitement as they ready their whaleboats. Running over to where they are letting down the boats, I quickly ask, "Can I help?"

"Here, take this line and pull!" yells one of the men.

Reaching up, I grab the rope, but it slips from my grip. One of the crew reaches around me and catches it and hands it back to me. Determined, I reach up and grab on again. This time I hold tight, nearly taking the skin off my hands, but I hold tight.

"Heave! Heave! Heave!" someone shouts.

The boats splash into the water, making them ready for the chase. The men shout with excitement as they row. Each boat has a man who stands in the bow with his sharp iron-barbed harpoon ready to throw.

The crew rows after a whale as it leads them on a chase across the water. I spot Jackson in the front set to heave his heavy harpoon.

My heart races as I hold my breath at the danger. It isn't easy, but finally, a harpoon is thrown. Again and again, more harpoons fly until one hits its target. The whale spouts blood immediately. One of the

185

crew next to me explains that means the iron had hit its vitals, as needed for the kill.

I hear Samuel yell, "We got you now!"

The whale races in a flurry across the water, pulling the whaleboat full of men behind. I hear their cheers of excitement as they ride the great whale that's hooked to the end of their rope. What an intoxicating thrill they must be having as the boat skids across the water. Then the giant whale raises its fluke into the air and descends into the depths. The water becomes quiet as the men wait. There's a man in the front of the boat ready with an ax.

"Watch that man with the ax," says James. "He's waiting to cut the rope if the whale should sound too deep. If it does, it could drag the boat down with the men in it."

I hold my breath and wait. But where did it go? Well, I can't hold my breath that long. It seems like an hour has gone by when all of a sudden it rises straight into the air with incredible force, nearly hitting the whaleboat. It dives and surfaces again and again. Each time another harpoon is thrown at the giant creature.

My heart pounds and I become sickened with the massive amount of blood from the slaughter. I guess I'm not ready for the brutality and pace the deck, watching, almost wishing the whale would break free from the harpoons and swim away. The creature is angry and has such fight in it, making the kill even harder. It's a slow death for the whale as the battle continues. For three hours, maybe four, it surfaces to breathe, only to find another harpoon ready to strike. Exhausted from the loss of blood, the angry giant struggles. Even though it's growing weak, the injured whale still has tremendous power and strength, and fights to live. The crew is exhausted, but they won't give up either. Who will win? The monster or the men?

The water has become bright red as the whale thrashes around. I notice something dark moving underwater between the ship and the whale.

I point at the shadows and ask, "What's that?"

"Those are sharks," the captain answers. "The smell of blood brings them in."

Just then the whale flips hard, crashing down its giant tail, hitting one of the boats. I hear screaming and look to see a man being tossed high into the air, to land in the bloody water.

Everyone starts yelling.

"Hurry, quick, grab him!" shouts one of the men.

"Pull him in!" hollers another.

"Grab the hook, and lay hold of him," yells another, while pointing at the giant hook.

"Make quick. Bring him back in the boat. Hurry!"

There is such frenzy in the bloody water as the sharks thrash around. It darkens even more from the red blood. The sharks are feasting on the whale, and this man is right in the midst of it all.

"Who is it?" I ask trembling.

"Samuel," says Captain Anthony, intently watching.

"Oh God!" I gasp.

I look, and he's right. I scan the boats for Samuel, but I don't see him. I look down at the sharks thrashing and Samuel's limp body being pulled under. I scream with fright and start to cry. We've already lost two men on this voyage. When will it stop?

I can't look. I run over by the cabin and collapse onto the deck. Burying my face into my hands, I sob. *"No, please, God, Not Samuel."*

When will this hellish voyage end? I agonize to myself.

I look over and see Preacher Man on his knees praying. I hope God is listening.

I hear the captain and the men screaming. "It's taking too long. Get him out of there!"

"He's a goner," I overhear someone say.

"They've got him!" someone yells.

But is he alive? I don't know. I don't want to know. I don't want to see. I just want to run away, but there's nowhere to run, there's nowhere to hide. Cupping my hands over my ears, I become terrified like a little girl again.

As I sit and sob, James comes over and puts his arm around me. "God, this is awful."

"He's dead, isn't he?" I cry. "I saw the sharks. I saw them pull him under. They've probably killed him." Burying my face on his chest, I cry uncontrollably.

Shhh," he whispers, holding me tight. "You're probably right, but there's nothing we can do about it. They're bringing him up now. I'll go see what I can find out."

I nod, trying to wipe away my tears. James walks over to the men laying Samuel's bloody, motionless body on the deck. All the crewmen gather around, blocking my view. Too frightened to look, I turn away.

Then James yells to me. "He's alive! He's moving!"

With my heart pounding, I stand up. But I'm afraid to look. I don't want to see the gruesome sight of how much the sharks have eaten. Captain Anthony and others are kneeling over Samuel so I still can't see. Waiting, wanting to know how bad it is, I feel fearful, not wanting to know if his arms or legs are gone.

Then James runs to me. "Adeleen, it's a miracle. He's all right."

I look over at Samuel and see him sitting up, sputtering and spitting, trying to recover from swallowing the seawater.

"Is he hurt?" I ask in a disbelieving voice.

"He doesn't seem to be. He got knocked unconscious from the whale's fluke and swallowed a whole lot of water when he fell in. He's lucky they fished him out so quickly before the sharks got to him. Damn lucky!"

Standing there wide-eyed, afraid to move, I tremble and sob with disbelief. I look out at the sharks feeding on the whale that's rolled on its back, a sure sign that it's dead. How is it possible Samuel lived through it all? I saw him being pulled underwater. How can it be that he's alive? Not able to wrap my head around it, I stand quiet and still. Then notice Preacher Man smiling at me. I nod my head and smile back. *God did answer his prayer.*

The crew hauls the whale to the side of the ship, securing it to be cut apart. The men on deck get back to work, busy, while laughing at what just happened. They must have been scared too as they watched it all and can joke now, but I know it's their way of dealing with the element of death and the dangers of whaling.

Together the men ready the ship to render the whale into valuable oil. On deck, large pots are sitting on bricks with fire, already hot and waiting to melt the blubber. This precious oil will be carried in barrels back to port in America. These men are happy, and this means money in their pockets. To them, it's well worth the danger. The black smoke rises high into the sky, causing a pillar of smoke that follows behind our ship, a sure sign we're a whaling ship.

Walking over to Samuel who's still sitting on the deck, I ask, "How are you?"

"That whale sure did ring my bell," he tells me as he rubs the back of his head.

"I was scared. I thought you died," I say, looking at him for reassurance.

"I tell ya, I didn't know nothin'. I didn't know what happened 'till they dropped me on the deck. Hell, they could have been a little gentler about it," he says as he continues to rub the back of his head.

"Samuel, I think you got that knot on your head from the whale, not the men," I assure him.

"That was a damn right angry whale. I've killed many a whale in my life, but this the first time one wanted to get even with me. I damn near lost," he says, shaking his head in disbelief.

I look at his tired, worn face, and all I can do is listen to him and be thankful he's still alive.

It takes three days to render the smelly whale down to seventy barrels of oil. The men work hard, and none shirk from their duties. They look forward to the money, the real reason they're on this ship.

Whatever's left of the whale's ghastly carcass is cut loose from the ropes and left to sink and feed the ocean.

Walking over to me, William, one of the oarsmen who had given chase, hands me a whale's tooth. Thanking him, I stand holding and staring at it. Like a tooth pulled from one of the prisoners, this tooth still has blood on it. I don't want it, but I have to take it. I don't want any reason for the crew to dislike me any more than they do.

Clutching it tightly in my hand, I think back to the whale's death. I remember how it fought so hard, leaping and thrashing, in the fight for its life, only to be chased to its death. Wrestling with my feelings, I remembered my struggles at the prison and my fight to survive. Life is hard, even for the creatures of the sea.

The whalers look at a whale's tooth as their prize, something they will make carvings on, a treasure they will take back home to their families.

"What have yah, girl?" asks James.

"A whale tooth," I say, showing it to him.

"It sure is a big one."

"Really big. What do you think I should do with it?"

"Just save it, Adeleen. It can remind you of your travels across this ocean on this here whaling ship."

"You mean a reminder of my life," thinking of the prison.

"Come on, let's join the others. You can show them your tooth," he says, beckoning me to join the group playing games.

"Only if I can cheat," I say with a smile.

❦❦❦❦❦

Back sailing again, it's clean-up time on the ship. Jackson is busy swabbing the deck, while others are scrubbing the giant iron pots. I'm thankful I don't have to scour them like I did the pots at the prison.

"What's that wretched smell?" I ask as the memories of the stink hole at the prison comes flooding back.

"Oh that, Miss?" asks Jackson.

"Yes, it smells like piss."

"It is, Miss," he replies with a big grin.

"What do you mean?" I ask aghast.

"It's the only thing that cuts the whale oil, and we need it to wash off the deck," he replies. "Haven't you seen the men when they go relieve themselves? They walk behind the whaleboat, over there where the bucket and barrels are." He points.

"Well, yes, but I thought they were just doing that over the side," I say sheepishly.

"No, Miss, they were filling up a bucket, and when that's full, they pour it into one of the giant barrels. They've been pissing in it ever since we left America and Australia."

Curious, James walks over to see what's making me so upset.

Glaring at him, I snap, "You been doing that in the bucket too?"

"Aye, why?" he asks.

My eyes widen as I look down at my wet bare feet. Horrified, I run to my berth to get my boots…another reason to dislike men.

"What's wrong with her?" I hear James asking as I run off.

"I don't know," answers Jackson, shaking his head.

❦❦❦❦❦

Today the wind is blowing strong, a sign another storm might be coming. I say might, because I don't always know. I sure hope so. Maybe it will wash the deck, and then I can go barefooted again.

With heavy winds in the sails, I picture a giant hand pushing our ship fast across the waters. I'm told the world is turning in our favor, which is a good thing. I'm glad the earth is round. If it were flat like they used to think it was, we'd probably be falling off it by now.

I feel the windy spray on my face as the ship races, crashing down with a great force on every wave, giving me a new challenge with new adventures. I'm not as afraid of the storms anymore, but feel strong and look forward to them. Until they get here...then I'm scared again. The riggings slap with a rhythmic sound against the mast as we ride the wind. Huge swells lift our ship high and then splash us down, only to rise again. As the ship tosses about on the rough sea, water sloshes over the deck. I'm very grateful for the ocean giving the boards a good cleaning.

Still, I haven't learned how to overcome all my fears, but I'm trying. One minute I feel strong, and the next, I'm reduced to a fearful child. So it is for me on the waves.

Using the privy is something I haven't gotten used to, especially when the ship is rocking hard from the giant waves. Sometimes I wish I had my own barrel up on deck in a little hideaway just for me. That way, there'd be no going below, although the men high up on the crosstrees would be able to see me. But still, it would make me feel a lot safer staying on the top deck, rather than passing by the crew. Although most seem friendly these days, still there are others who give me chills.

A few more of the crew have dropped their respect for me and don't care what they say or how they act. It's nothing new after being in prison, but I feel the isolation of being on a ship with only men, where some would get pleasure in throwing me overboard. I have no one to share my real feelings with or tell my worries and fears to.

I don't want to become weak; I want to take care of myself. I tire of someone watching my every move. Often the six Irishmen mingle with the crew, but other times, they stay together or go off by themselves. I know they're watching out for me the best they can, especially James, but I still miss my friends back in Fremantle. If only this giant piece of wood would make port somewhere, if only for a little while.

Coming from below, I walk over to sit on deck against the rails. James is looking up as Thomas and Martin try to learn how to climb up to the mast. Putting my hands up to shade my eyes from the glare of the sun, I can't help but shake my head in disbelief. They're unsure and unsteady, ribbing each other about who's the bravest.

Heckling the two, James yells, "Yer toes aren't long enough!"

The crewmen who climb the towering mast are barefoot or wear soft-soled shoes, making it easier to curl their toes to hang on.

Shaking his head 'No' and chuckling loudly, Thomas is the first to give up.

"It's harder than me thinks," he tells us. "And that there mast, I was afraid I'd break me neck if I lost me grip. Aye, it sure is swaying right big up there," he says out of breath.

James slaps his back. "Good work! You did yer best!"

"Aye, why don't you have a go?" Thomas encourages.

Chuckling James shakes his head. Then both walk over to sit by me.

The three of us watch Martin. He seems determined to conquer his quest and continues higher up the mast. Making it to the crosstree, he stops and looks down at us. We can see he's hanging on for dear life.

I wave at him and he smiles. Not wanting to let go, he doesn't wave back. I wonder what it's like up there as the ship sways back and forth.

One of the crew beckons him to try to walk out on the crossbeam, but I see his head motion a definite 'No!' He's had enough and quickly scrambles back down.

With applause from us for his feat, he holds his chest a little higher as he comes to join us. He says the crew makes it look easy, but it's not.

I'm amazed how the Irish are fitting in and finding common ground with the crew, which takes some of the tension away.

33

Before going to the captain's cabin when I need a fresh dress, I always give him a nod to signal my intent, and he nods back. Today I notice him watching me more than usual. Moving to the door that leads into his cabin, I look back at him and wonder what he's thinking.

Entering the room, I remind myself that this is such a fine thing the captain has done giving all of this to me. Slowly I open the trunk and gaze within at all the many dresses I have to choose among.

Sitting on the floor, I decide, today I want to take everything from the trunk and look at them one at a time.

I must have taken hours touching each treasure that lay before me. I've had so little in my life, and now so much. It is only in a dream that I would be so gifted.

Looking farther into the trunk, I find the blue slippers that match the blue dress I'm wearing. I brush the dirt off my bare feet and slip them on. Giggling, I wiggle my toes. My feet have never known such dainty shoes like these before; they feel so foreign. Then I remember, again, in the past, how I got my boots from dead people. The strangeness of it all. Although these weren't directly taken off of someone dead, still someone died. Maybe I'll get something new when I get to America.

Thinking more about the prior captain's wife and how she must have been a beautiful lady, I imagine her wearing these things. It's quite evident her husband provided well for her by the clothes she had worn. How sad for the prior captain to have her die in childbirth, and his child at the same time.

I remembered my pain when my baby Rose was born, then taken from me. My grief has never left me and probably never will. Still, I know how I felt being a mum, even if it was for just a short while.

Looking deeper to the bottom of the trunk, I find an image of a lady pressed onto tin. This must be her, the one who died. Just as I imagine, she's beautiful. While I'm gazing at the picture, Captain Anthony comes through the door.

"Oh! I'm sorry, Miss Adeleen. I thought you were gone."

"No, I'm sorry, I've taken too long. I just wanted to sit for a while and look at all the lovely things you gave me."

Holding up the tin, I ask, "Did you know this was in here?"

"I didn't, I've never seen the contents of the trunk," he says as he takes the picture from my hand. He gazes at it for a moment, then says, "I'd like to make sure the former captain gets this, if you don't mind."

Nodding my head, I agree.

I notice a sadness in his voice. I want to ask what's making him feel this way, but maybe another time would be better.

"I'll leave and let you continue as you are," he tells me.

"No, I think I've enjoyed enough for today." I stand and close the lid.

Aware of his sensitivity, and seeing another side of this man, I'm drawn to him even more than before. He is handsome, bold, and strong, but yet he is soft when he speaks about the former captain and his wife. Does Captain Anthony have someone in his life? He hasn't said.

I hesitate, which seems like a very long moment, and then tell him, "I'll save more for another time."

As I step towards the door, he reaches for me. Does he dare? Pulling me close, I don't push him away. He leans in and kisses me- ...ever so softly. A tingle passes through my whole body. I can't help myself and melt into his kiss. I've haven't been with a man who I wasn't forced to be with. Never have I had a choice to stay or go. Right now, everything within me says to stay, and nothing within my heart tells me to go.

Letting go of me, I watch as he walks over and lights a lantern, giving his room a beautiful glow from the warm flickering light.

He turns and stands for a moment looking at me. Trying to find reassurance on his face, I'm paralyzed as he walks back over to me. Kissing me again, he slowly begins to unbutton my dress. I remove his jacket from his shoulders and begin to unbutton his shirt revealing his magnificent muscles, which I knew were hiding.

Kissing me ever so gently on my bare shoulder, he drops my dress to the floor. I feel his breath on my skin as he inhales to take me away. For the first time in my life, I choose and freely give into my desires.

❧❧❧❧❧

Slipping out of his room late in the night while he is sleeping, I sneak back to my own bed, not knowing if I should stay with him. It would be awkward for me and him if the crew were to see me leave.

The next morning I'm at a loss on how to act around him. Feeling uncomfortable, I stay away, far away from him, trying to avoid eye contact throughout most of the day.

Am I ashamed? No, I don't think so. I just don't know what to expect. I don't want to feel like I belong to someone again, just because we joined. So I stay busy, mending the sails or helping Peat. A couple of times, I look up in his direction and see him watching me.

Oh, what have I done? I can't do this again. I mustn't.

As the day goes on, I begin to feel more relaxed. Occasionally I notice a smile from him, but I think we both want it to stay our secret, and so it does.

Enjoying the sun set with James and the others, I wonder if they know what happened last night? Is there talk? They were playing cards and drinking, so maybe not.

The sky is turning pink as the sun begins to dip into the ocean and the heavens paint a blush of violet across the sky. I hear soft music coming from the captain's room. Peace settles across the ship from the music that can be heard by most all. It's as if he is putting the ship and everyone to sleep.

I look out at the quiet ocean waters that are changing to a deep, dark blue again, and feel a restful calm as the music moves across the deck.

"I didn't know the captain could play the violin," says James.

"He does that some nights. It's been some time since he's played on those strings. Sometimes we wonder what he's got holed up inside himself," says Samuel.

"I like it," says Jackson, leaning back against the rails and puffing on his pipe.

"I do too," I say. I like it a lot. Am I the reason for the beautiful, soft music?

❧❧❧❧❧❧

This ship has a dark side. I can't quite figure it out, but I'm told by one of the crew that a ghost that lives on board. Sometimes I think the men say things just to scare me, but they have planted a seed of fear within me. Am I jumpy? Hell yes. That's just how I am. I jump if someone comes up behind me unexpectedly. I jump at loud crashes. Let's just say I'm easy to scare.

I also find myself looking over my shoulder, not always, but enough — especially knowing there are some on board who don't want me here.

I remember one time when I went below and felt a cold chill run down my spine. It reminded me of the ghost down the steps at the prison that Rou and I felt. But on this ship there are eyes watching, watching me all the time. At times I think I see something in the dark shadows, but when I stare at it, trying to adjust my eyes, whatever it is, is gone. Has the same ghost I felt at the prison followed me onto the ship? I hope not.

I was used to the stares from the guards and male prisoners at the prison, but I feel it's more dangerous here because there's no place to escape. I'm getting tired of not feeling safe, and today is no different as my uneasiness grows more intense. I can't explain it, but I sense danger.

This is a different kind of survival for me. At least at the prison, I didn't feel like I could be thrown overboard to drown. I just need to be careful. No telling how much longer our journey will be.

It's been months already, and the days all seem to blend into each other. I'm so disgustingly bored and almost wish for a storm, at least then the crew would be kept busy, and I'd have something to do.

My days seem long, yet the ship never stops traveling north across the sea. It's getting darker as the sun hides behind the water's edge. Crimson glows across the sky as another endless day slips into darkness. Another day closer to America.

Early, just before sunrise I hear someone shout, "FIRE! FIRE! There's fire in the lower deck!" There's a lot of commotion as the men run for buckets, throwing them over the side of the ship to fill with water and hauling them back to take below. I can smell smoke as the men form a line, handing bucket after bucket to each other. They scream and yell, "Faster! Faster, get more water!"

With men running past me, almost knocking me down, I back up to stay out of their way.

It happens so fast. Someone grabs me, putting a hand over my mouth, dragging me away into the dark shadows of the stowed rowboats, away from everyone. Kicking violently, I try to get loose, and then someone punches me in the jaw. I'm dazed but still somewhat conscious as two men quickly gag me so I can't make a sound. They tie me in the heavy wooden chair, and there I sit unable to scream.

The fire is their diversion, so I don't think anyone even notices what's happening to me. James is busy helping the crew fighting the fire, so it was easy for these two to grab me.

Well, they found a plan that finally works. Within moments they push the chair and me overboard. The last thing I remember seeing before going over the side of the ship is the two men smiling at each other.

I hit the night's black water hard, face first, stunning me, but I remain conscious. The chair rolls and I'm above water struggling to breathe. Water quickly soaks the gag they've tied around my mouth.

198

Inhaling through my nose the splashing waves of water, I know…I'm going to die.

Wave upon wave beats at me as I struggle. They've tied me so tight, but still, with my strong desire to survive, I struggle to breathe and free myself.

"I got ya," Christian yells as he grabs the chair before it can float past him. Quickly he ties it to a rope, tethered it to the ship, then reaches around and tries to remove my gag.

Fearful and wide-eyed, I look at him and can't believe my eyes as I continue to struggle to breathe.

Christian says, "Let me untie you. Stop struggling."

That's easy for him to say; he's not drowning. Finally loosening my gag, he pulls it away from my mouth.

"You have to stop wiggling," he demands. "I can't untie you unless you hold still."

I close my eyes and force myself to stop struggling. Then I feel my hands freed, and reach up grabbing tightly onto Christian.

Shaking and struggling to get my breath, I sputter, "Thank you, thank you, thank you."

The dawning sky is already starting to lighten. Too far from the ship for anyone to hear us, together, we cling to the chair. Christian says it should only be minutes before someone spots us.

"I know Mopsy will be up on the crosstree, so he'll see us. Just don't you fret, Miss. I won't let go of you."

Shaken and cold, I can barely nod, yes. Christian holds me tight, and I him.

Then he tells me he saw the two men grab me, and with little time, he grabbed hold of a rope tied to the side of the ship from whaling and jumped. He hit the water ahead of me, hoping the chair would float in his direction.

As the sky awakens, sure enough, we see the commotion on the ship as they spot us.

How stupid those men are that threw me overboard. Didn't they know the chair wouldn't sink? Wood floats, you dumb arses! But I guess I'd be long gone if it hadn't been for Christian.

Soon we hear voices yelling from the ship.

"The ship's dragging something off the stern, sir," hollers Mopsy above on the mast.

"What is it?" Captain Anthony asks.

"I don't know, captain. There's something's attached to one of the ropes tied to the aft of the ship," Mopsy hollers.

Lifting his spyglass, the captain looks and yells, "What the hell? Quick, pull it in!"

As the men pull the heavy rope, their eyes widen with amazement. There we are, two people desperately clinging onto something tied to the rope. Pulling quickly, more and more men come to help.

"It's the lady," says one of the crew, "and Christian," says another. "What are they doing?"

"Good God, it's Adeleen," screams James.

"And Christian," shouts another.

"Get them up here!" Captain yells, as they work together to bring us back on board.

All the crew, including the two who threw me overboard, are helping to bring us back on board. I see the two looking at each other, probably thinking I don't know it's them, and just maybe I wouldn't be able to identify them. It had been dark when they'd grabbed me from behind. But, fortunately I got a good look. They're unaware that I know how to burn faces into my memory.

Climbing over the rail, James reaches out and helps pull me on board. "Are you all right? What happened? How did you and Christian end up in the water?"

Too weak to answer, I grab tightly onto James and start to cry uncontrollably.

Kneeling down in front of Christian and me, the captains asks, "What happened here?"

Slowly the crew pulls the old wooden chair back up onto the deck. Looking at the chair, and then at the two men, Christian struggles to get to his feet wanting to grab Wylie.

George stops him and pulls him away. "You're in no condition to tangle with him, mate."

Exhausted, I lie on the deck. Lifting my arm, I point at Drissel. James holds me as I struggle to tell how the two of them threw me overboard.

Christian, out of breath, says, "It's Wylie and Drissel. They're the ones who threw her overboard."

He tells the captain that he could see what was going to happen when he saw the two men tying me to the chair. They were already pushing the chair and me overboard. He says he didn't think he'd have time to yell, so he grabbed the rope and jumped. He had to be quick, or else the chair and I would be lost.

"Take them below and put 'em in irons," yells the captain. "I'll deal with them later." Then he kneels in front of me, brushing my wet hair away from my face. "I could have lost you," he says as he looks at me. "Peat, take her below. She has a gash on her forehead that needs seeing too."

"Aye, Captain."

James looks at me stunned, probably wondering why the captain said what he did. While the captain walks Christian to his cabin to question him more, I don't say anything, but just lie exhausted, cradled safely in James's arms as he and Peat take me below. Cold and frightened, I can't stop shaking.

Behind us I hear the Drissel and Wylie yelling. "She's bad luck! She'll take us down to the graveyard below! She will! We need to send her to the deep!" yells Drissel as his hands are tied behind him.

"She don't belong on our ship," Wylie hollers as he's also tied. "You'll all see. She'll bring the witch to take us all."

I still hear them as the men shove them down the steps to the lower deck. "She's is a witch!" are the last words I make out.

The rest of the crew glares at me. I can see in their eyes and wonder if they think Drissel and Wylie are right.

34

The winds are blowing strong today, pushing the ship at a fast pace. It has taken a few days for me to recover from being thrown in the ocean.

James tells me they say it should be less than a month, depending on the winds, until we make port in America.

I don't know if I can last another month. I don't even want to go down below to sleep anymore. I'm too afraid. Instead, I choose to sleep on deck. There I don't feel so trapped, even though that's where Drissel and Wylie grabbed me, but still, I feel safer up top. I'm uneasy around the crew. James sleeps on deck, staying close. I get the sense he believes it's his fault that he didn't notice I was missing. I think this Irishman wants to be my protector but feels he's failed. Making up for it, he tries to stay where he can see me at all times. But still, I don't trust any of the men on this ship anymore. Well, maybe James, Peat, Christian, and the captain, I do. But the rest? I don't know.

"Adeleen, are you doing all right today?" asks Jackson, walking over to where I'm standing watching the water.

Quickly James comes over to see why he's talking to me.

"I'm better. I hope that's the last time I taste that awful saltwater," I say, trying to make light of it.

"Us crew couldn't believe it when we saw you and Christian on that chair," says Jackson.

"It's a good thing it didn't sink," says Christian as he walks over, joining us.

I look at James, who has an annoying frown on his face.

"Aye," I say.

"Adeleen, do you want to come a bit and sit over here with me while I untangle some ropes?" asks James.

"I'd like that," I say as I walk away with him.

I know James is trying to put his protective barrier around me. It's all right for now, but I don't need him hovering all the time, I need to breathe and be myself, even though things are pretty scary for me on board. I don't want him to smother me.

I stay by James as he piles ropes, Scraps comes over and puts his head on my lap, wanting me to pet him. He's become my friend on this trip, although I wish he had been there when the men were tying me to the chair. Maybe he could have bitten them.

I notice Captain Anthony staying busy. Is he's losing control of his men on this ship? It's got to be a hard job keeping everyone from killing each other, and me.

⁂

Most of the month has passed, and our ship is delayed by several more whale hunts. Hearing yelling, I walk over to see what it's all about.

"Well, the captain, in his fancy suit, needs to quit all this whaling stuff, and get us to America, or just drop us at the nearest port so we can get off this water log!" James yells in a slurred voice while staring angrily at the captain.

"All good and fine, Mr. Wilson, but it cost a hell of a lot of money for us to sail all the way to Australia to fetch you. So if we need to whale to get some of the money to pay for your sorry asses, then we'll whale," the captain says staring back at him.

James' face is red, his hair unkempt, and he's having trouble keeping his balance. It's clear he is drunk. He's been heavy into the rum lately, and I don't like him when he's this way. I know he's frustrated because it's taking longer than we all thought to get to America, although the captain's right. But when James is drunk all he wants to do is pick a fight.

Shaking his fist, James yells, "And another thing." He points at me. "You need to stay away from Adeleen. I see you looking at her."

Uh-oh. "You need never mind that," I quickly tell James as I tug at his arm trying to lead him away. Looking back at Captain Anthony, I shake my head.

Thomas helps me to walk James over by the rail to sit on the deck, but it isn't long before he's lying down passed out.

I've decided to go down in the galley and sit and talk with Peat. Working in the kitchen with him, I feel pretty safe. I'm able to give him some ideas of how we cooked at the prison. I tell him how I went out to dig potatoes to bring back so we could boil them. Peat looks at me, and I can tell he feels sorry for me. But I tell him, no, that's what I wanted to do. I wanted to get outside the walls, so I chose to go dig. He shakes his head. Maybe I'd better not tell him too much about my life at the prison. I don't think he can handle hearing some of it.

Maybe I'll tell him about the bull that visited our kitchen instead; he should like that story.

Peat has little choice but to serve the same food day after day. Still, I learn a lot from listening to him. He's been cooking on ships for many years, although he won't tell me how many. He quit counting long ago.

We're lucky we got fresh fruit when we found that island. Most of the men like the rum and beer, which are keeping them content.

I don't understand why these men choose life at sea and the dangerous life of whaling. Maybe I'm just looking at it from a woman's view.

Peat and I hear the ship's bell ringing non-stop, which means all hands on deck. I take a deep breath and think, *What now?*

As I start to follow Peat up on deck with everyone else, I hear Andrews calling for Scraps.

"Can't you find him?" I ask.

"No, I think he's gone farther below. I need to find him. Can you help me?"

"Sure," I say as I start calling for the dog.

I know Scraps likes me, so he'll probably come when he sees me. Calling for him, we go even further down the steps to the lowest level of the ship where the cargo is held.

"Sometimes he likes to go down here to chase rats," says Andrews.

Suddenly, behind me, I hear the door bolt. I quickly turn to see Andrews locking it. Over against the wall, Wylie and Drissel are chained to the ship. A cold, icy fear floods my body, and I scream, hoping someone will hear me. I yell at Andrews, "Why are you locking the door? What are you doing? We're supposed to go up on deck. Let's go back up," I plead.

Fear grips me, and I wish James were here. Where is he when I need him? Then I remember, he's passed out drunk on deck.

⁂

"Didn't you hear the bell ringing? We need to go up on deck," I frantically tell Andrews, while glancing over at the two men chained to the wall.

"Aye, get her," says Drissel with a disgusting grin.

"We'll give a hand, mate. Just let us loose," says Wylie.

"Help me!" I scream, hoping someone will hear. "What are you doing?"

"You'll find out," he says with his eyes fixed on me.

Wylie and Drissel laugh as they watch.

There must be so much chaos up on deck that no one hears my cries. Maybe James will notice I'm missing and come looking. I bet Andrews created the diversion so everyone will gather up top, trying to figure out who and why the bell signaled an alarm.

My eyes widen with fear. Desperately I yell for help again.

"You're gonna like what I'm gonna do to you," he says with a sinister smile as he unbuckles his belt.

"Hey," say the Wylie and Drissel as they get excited. "Unlock us. We'll help you, mate."

Walking to the back of the hold, Andrews releases a lever, causing seawater to flow in. I run for the bolted door, trying to open it, but I'm not strong enough to unlatch it.

Seeing the water, Drissel yells, "What the hell you doing there, mate? Are you trying to scuttle the ship?"

"Shut up," Andrews growls back.

Wylie cries out frantically, "Wait! What are you doing? Why are you letting the water in?"

"Oh, this? It's gonna to take some time, but I'll have all the time in the world just for her and me," he says glaring at me.

He's making no sense. Backing up, trying to stay just out of his reach, I realizing he's not going to unchain Drissel and Wylie, and everyone on ship is probably going to drown.

The two men realize it too and start shouting. Hopefully, now maybe someone will hear us.

"You can't get away, and no one can help you," Andrews tells me. "You're all mine. You think you can walk around this ship looking the way you do and not make us want you? You're just like all the other bitches I've known. They liked teasing me too. No! You're more like my mama. She flaunted herself in front of men, too. I was little, and I hid and watched what they did to her. You're a whore just like her. You flaunt your body, and make us look at you. I'm going to give you what you're asking for," he says with his sick smile.

With him talking like a madman, I continue to back up trying to stay out of his reach.

The crew has heard us and are pounding on the door, yelling for us to unlock it. By now they must see the water seeping under the door. Backing up farther, I glance towards the door. Suddenly, I run for it again, but before I can reach it, Andrews grabs hold of me and wraps his arm around my waist. Kicking and screaming, I pound my fist into his face and poke at his eyes, until he loosens his grip for just a second, long enough for me to jump away. He reaches for me again but misses. The water is getting deeper, and it's harder to stay away from him.

"Why the water?" I ask.

"It don't matter much," he says, with the demonic look still on his face. "We both belong in the deep."

I look boldly at him. "I've been raped before, so you're not the first. But why do you want to drown the crew? Your mates?"

"Oh, it's just water. It won't hurt, and shouldn't take long. It will wash away our sins, then together we can go. Maybe everything will get better then."

He isn't making sense. I've seen many demon-possessed minds in prison, and he definitely has one.

Remembering I still carry my rusty knife, I pull it from my waist belt and hold it where he can't see it. As he lunges for me, I shove it into his chest. Stunned, he stops for a moment, then reaches up and grabs at his chest, pulling out the knife and throwing it into the rising water. Glaring at me, he lunges. Screaming, I run for the door again.

Glancing at his chest, he wipes his hand across his blood-soaked shirt. "Oh, this ain't stopping me, young lady, you'll have to do better than this," he says as he grabs hold of me again.

"Please, I don't want to die," I plead kicking and screaming. "I'll give you what you want, just stop the water, please, I beg you."

With the cold seawater almost to our knees, I wrestle with him. He's much taller than I am, and easily overpowers me. Scratching at his face, he changes his hold on me, and grabs my hair, pulling me with him. But still I fight.

Spotting a table, he drags me towards it. Using one arm to shove everything off, he throws me on it.

Screaming and kicking, I'm determined not to let him have me. I know how to fight, and I've had plenty of practice in the prison. Like Preacher Man told me, although I don't know where the words come from, but I whisper a prayer: "Please, God. Help me."

With my free hand, I scratch at his eyes again and bite. He struggles, wrestling with me. Then he gives me a swift punch to my jaw, and I fall limp, pretending to be knocked out. Ripping at the bodice of my dress, he runs his hand across my chest. Seeming more agitated, it's obvious he doesn't want me unconscious but wants me fully awake for what he's about to do.

Slapping my face, he tries to awaken me, but I continue to stay limp in his grasp. I know the wound in his chest will continue to bleed heavily and slow him down.

Suddenly, I feel his grip loosen and I push him away. Surprised, he falls back into the water.

Rolling off the table to the other side, I keep my distance from him all while the gaping hole in Andrews chest bleeds more. I know I have to keep fighting if I'm going to live. Seeing the blood drain from his body, I know it's just a matter of time.

"This has to happen. You have to die with me," he says slowly as he fights to stay conscious. But it's no use. He falls helplessly, face down in the water.

Loud banging continues as the crewmen try desperately to break through the door. They have no way of knowing what's going on.

Demanding for someone to unlock the door, I yell back "I can't, it's too heavy."

The crew starts to chop at the door with an ax, and soon there's a small hole they can look through.

Wylie yells to them, "There's water coming in. Hurry! Get the door open."

Finally they pull the door apart and squeeze through. The crew wades through the water, pushing aside floating cargo.

Someone yells, "Make a bucket line and bring in the pump. Hurry men, we don't have much time."

I hear Wylie and Drissel trying to convince the crew to unlock them so they can help.

Captain Anthony yells, "We have to close the lever and seal off the intake. Someone unchain the prisoners. We don't want them to drown.

Oh, yes I do.

The captain's first concern is the water. Hurrying to the intake, he and the others work desperately to stop the incoming flow.

"What the bloody hell happened? Adeleen, are you all right?" asks James as he wades over to me.

Once the water slows to a trickle, Captain looks over at me and see's Jackson taking Andrews limp body from my arms. I had pulled him from the water, not really wanting him to down.

Appearing stunned, Captain asks, "What's happened?"

My body becomes clammy and cold. Confused, I sit quiet as James wraps a blanket around my shoulders. The trauma is more than I can handle.

Hanging my head, all I can do is cry. Falling apart, I say, "I don't know! I don't know! I can't find a safe place anywhere. I should never have come on this ship. It was safer for me at the prison. At least there, they didn't want to kill me. This is all a mistake. I shouldn't have come and should have stayed in prison."

Looking across the room, I see Wylie and Drissel being released from their chains, and hate them.

James grabs my arms and says, "Adeleen! It will be all right. Don't let this take your freedom away. You're free now, and we're almost to America. Yes, there are still bad people out there, but there are also those you can trust — many more who won't hurt you. Adeleen, look at me, look around," he says as he gives me a shake. "You have to believe me, I know you're strong. This scum is cruel, and sick."

Confused over everything, including my feelings for Captain Anthony and James, I shake my head "no," and bury my face in his chest, crying.

"Oh, Adeleen, don't give up. You'll find what I'm telling you is true. Please don't give up your new life. We're almost there. Adeleen, America is waiting for you. There we can put our past behind us and make a new start." Squeezing me tightly, James holds me close. "Did he hurt you?" he asks softly.

"No, I've had thirteen years of training to deal with a man like him," I say sadly. "I know he wasn't in his right mind. He has his demons, but I think today they lost."

My thoughts make me wonder. *Will this ship ever find land again? Will I live to see it?*

Taking me up on deck, James tells me, "They've stopped the water coming in and are holding Andrews below in another confined area, along with Wylie and Drissel, so you don't need to worry. Andrews has lost so much blood that they're not sure if he will live."

So, my knife has done it again. It's rusty, so infection is sure to make short work of him. Have I killed another? How many does that make, and how many more will there be? When will I ever stop?

35

We've been at sea for most of five months — we have to be getting close to America. Depressed, I choose to isolate myself down in the galley by Peat. I've worn the same dress for five days now and have no desire to change, even though I can smell my own body odor.

James stays close looking into the galley often to see if I'm here, but I find myself retreating internally, wanting to shut him and the world out.

Traveling north in Atlantic Ocean, we head to port in at New Bedford harbor, in the state of Maine. James and the other Fenians are arguing with Mr. Breslin and Captain Anthony. They're demanding the ship make port so we can be put off as soon as possible. Like me, they feel the ship is a prison. We want to be free, but we can't feel that way on ship. Only on land, then maybe, we can.

The arguing soon quells, and the evening brings laughter as the crew tells stories of their adventures at sea. I sit in a lonely spot away from everyone and listen. I see James across the deck. He knows I want to be left alone, so he's giving me time.

The captain stays away also. He watches me, but keeps his distance. He must see me struggling. Why doesn't he say something to me? Was I just his whore for that one night?

❦❦❦❦❦❦

Everyone is aware this will be our last few days on ship. I'm sure they can't wait to get home.

This morning I don't feel so well. The sea isn't rough, but the motion seems to affect me more than usual. Trying to get to my feet, I stumble and fall to my knees. What's happening? I'm dizzy. Am I seasick after all this time? I sure don't feel very well. In fact, I feel awful.

Noticing something's not right, James asks, "What's wrong?" But as soon as he takes a good look at me, he sees I'm pale.

"I'll get you to the rail," he says leading me across deck. "You feel mighty hot too."

Looking at my hand, I pick at it. It's red and swelling from where I accidentally cut myself with my rusty knife.

"What's the matter with her?" Captain Anthony asks James.

"I don't know. She's sick and I think she might have a fever," says James, looking at me worried.

"I cut my hand with my rusty knife when I was fighting Andrews a few days ago. It's starting to hurt. It must have a little piece of metal in it. I can't get it out, and now it's starting to swell." I tell them both.

"You mustn't let anything like that stay in there. It's dangerous," says James.

"Here, let me see," says Captain. He takes my hand to look closer, then sees the red line going up my arm. "Come with me," he says,
lifting me in his arms and carrying me towards the galley.

"What's going on? Where the bloody hell are you taking her?" James demands, following close behind.

"Where are you taking me?" I scream, trying to wiggle out of his arms.

"Stop it!" he says firmly. "I'm getting help. I'm trying to save your life. Cook! Cook, where are you?"

Peat comes through the door into the galley.

"She's got the streak," says Captain Anthony.

"Here, sit up here," Peat says clearing a place on his chopping block. Reluctantly scooting onto the block, I let Peat take my hand. Looking at my cut, he says, "We have to get what's imbedded out. I'll burn the knife."

"What knife? Another knife? No! Oh no, you're not. It'll be fine," I say while trying to climb down.

"Stop, you have to let Cook remove it. You've got poison in your blood, and we have to stop it. It will kill you, Adeleen," says Captain Anthony.

Well, isn't that something? All this time I'm trying to protect myself from others, and I may end up killing myself.

Working in the prison hospital, I've seen many with the red curse, and I know it could mean death. But I try to convince myself he must be wrong and disagree. "No, it will be all right, I just need to wash it more."

"You're so hard headed." Captain Anthony lifts my arm, pointing, "You see that red line on your arm? Soon it will go all the way up, and when it does, it will go into your body and kill you."

Peat nods, and James looks scared. Looking at my hand again and then at the red-hot knife that Peat's holding, I pull away. Not feeling well, I still have the fight to argue.

"You've got to be kidding," I say, shaking my head no while looking at Peat with my pitiful face.

"You have to let them do this," pleads James. "You'll be patched up and feeling better before you know it."

"Maybe we can wait to see what it looks like tomorrow."

"No, I'm telling you, you need it out right now," argues Captain.

I look again at Peat, knowing he's right, "Ohh…no," I mutter. I give a big swallow and a great big sigh, and then say, "This is really going to hurt, isn't it?

"I'm afraid so," he says.

Looking at Peat, I narrow my eyes. "You'd better not hurt me any more than you have to."

From the looks on both of their faces, I think I might have scared them. I lie down on the block and put my hand out.

Peat gives me a leather strap to bite on as I look away from my hand and into James's worried blue-green eyes. In just moments I feel the red-hot knife probe my hand as Peat tries to get the rusty metal out.

God, this hurts! But, I try not to scream, thinking back to how brave Rou was when Dr. Ross stitched her. With my eyes fixed on James, I feel the intense pain of the hot knife as Peat digs deeper to find the metal. Great drops of sweat start running down my face. Nearly biting through the leather strap, I close my eyes, taking my thoughts back to the prison, to some of the horrific experiences I've had to endure and think. "This is nothing."

Gritting my teeth into the leather strap, I can no longer stay silent and let out a high-pitched muffled scream and tightly grip James's hand, nearly twisting it from his arm. The captain holds my other arm straight as Peat finds the rusty piece of metal.

Finally, it's over, and he's got it.

"She's got the poison real bad," says Peat.

Putting a hot rag on my hand, he wraps it. "I'll put some draw on it so it can help pull the poison. We'll have to change it sometime tonight before you go to sleep. Sorry if I hurt you, Miss."

I smile back at him and say softly, "Thank you, Peat."

He looks at me, then at the captain and James, and together we're all glad it's over.

⁂

I'm told we're just a day or two from port in America, but I'm not getting any better. I'm actually getting worse. Barely able to lift my head, I lie on a blanket on the deck.

The captain's holding my blue comb in his hand. Looking down at me, he brushes some hair that's in my face to one side and gently tucks in the comb securely. I see James glaring at him and know it must take everything in him not to argue. Well, that's something.

The captain leans over me, putting his cheek to mine. I can smell him and feel his soft beard on my skin next to my cheek. He softly whispers in my ear, "I'm sorry, Adeleen. I'm so sorry."

"What's going to happen?" I murmur. "Am I going to die? Are you going to bury me at sea like the others?"

Not waiting for his answer, I close my eyes and dream about my blue comb and how Mychael had roughly carved it from the old piece of wood that found its way to the sandy shores by the prison. It was another lifetime ago when he'd told me how a blue tree from a faraway land must have fallen into the sea and washed ashore in Australia. It had to drift across the deep waters of the ocean before it could be made into something so beautiful. He'd carved it with me in mind, to bring me a tiny bit of joy. I treasure my comb. In a way, it somehow reminds me of my life, reflecting my struggles.

Moaning with fever, I fall in and out of trapped memories that are forever burned in my mind. Those thoughts hold me captive as I find no rest. I want to dream of America and make new memories, but instead, many are my nightmares from the past.

It's cooler on deck. I see some of the crew gather around watching as Peat dips a cloth in cold water and hands it to James to put on my brow. Ever so gently, they try to bring down my fever. I smile faintly. All this attention, I'm a lucky girl.

"How long until we make port?" I hear James ask Samuel.

"About a day and a half, if the wind holds."

Then the captain announces, "Change in plans, we're not porting north in New Bedford, Maine. We're going into New York harbor. We'll save a day. Make course change, Mr. Smith."

"Aye, Captain."

I hear cheers from the men as they adjust the giant sails to head due west.

Looking up in desperate need, the captain pounds on the mast. "Come on, come on, you blasted wind. Blow harder!"

Everyone can see the anguish he's feeling. Grabbing one of the crew by the shirt he says, "Tighten the ropes, and put more into the sails. We have to make her go faster."

Is he afraid he's losing me? I notice the men climbing high on the rigging, but I think they are only making themselves look busy for him, when all the while they know it won't go any faster. They have already done everything they can to make the ship move.

Somewhat delirious, I smile and think back in my memory how the oarsmen pulled the ship with ropes. I don't think they want to row all the way to New York.

The sounds of the creaking and snapping of the ship's masts and water lapping the sides of the ship echo in my head. Even the men talking among themselves seems loud and makes me unsettled.

"She's gonna die, you know. No one gets well when they have the red line," say one of them.

"No! She's a fighter, she won't let that happen," says another.

"It's a shame. She's come so far only to die."

I open my eyes and faintly see them through a cloud, but hear them perfectly.

"Maybe if we were to lighten the load," one of them says.

"Yea, that might help," says another, "but it will take a miracle to get us there any sooner."

My eyes follow as one of the crewmen walks over to Samuel, leaning to whisper in his ear. What's he telling him?

Samuel walks over to the captain and whispers in his ear as well. Both captain and Samuel nod in agreement.

Samuel then walks back over to the crew. "Throw what you can overboard. See if you can lighten the load," he orders.

"What about the whale oil we've gotten on board? Should we throw that over too?" one asks, knowing it means money in their pockets.

Samuel thinks for a moment and then walks over to Captain Anthony, Mr. Breslin and Mr. Desmond, knowing it's their decision. This ship is to recoup some of its cost of this trip by whaling. I see the three men putting their heads together.

Then captain yells to Samuel, "Some, but not all. So what if we get to port with less than we should? They don't know how much we have on ship."

It must not matter much at this point; everyone is eager to make port in America.

Listening to the crew, I realize I was wrong. Not all of them wish me dead. Some of them really do like me. James had told me anyone of them would be proud if I had taken a liking to them, but I didn't believe him. I now know there are good men on this ship, something I seldom saw at the prison. Sadly, I've learned to mistrust all men. But now, at last, I'm seeing them differently. They're not all bad after all.

216

Well into the late afternoon I lie quietly on deck. Weak, not wanting to move, I hear Peat. "Her fever seems to be dropping," he says as he puts a cool cloth on my forehead.

I can't help but moan as I move slightly.

"You'll be all right," Peat tells me.

"You think she's better?" asks James.

"No, her infection is still real bad, and she could still die," whispers Peat, thinking I can't hear.

Trying to lift my head, slowly I open my eyes, only to close them again.

"Hold on, we're almost there. We're almost to your new home, almost to America. Hold on, Adeleen," pleads James.

Delirious, I have such a headache and moan from the discomfort. I just want quiet. Feeling the cooling damp cloths that James and Peat put to my brow helps. I love them both.

"Land ahoy!" yells Mopsy on the mast above.

I try to sit up. I want to see America. Unable to, I collapse back down. "Help me," I murmur, "I want to see!"

James takes one arm and the captain the other and try to help me to stand. I'm too lightheaded and start to pass out. Lying me back down, I close my eyes for a moment.

"I want to see America," I mumble again. "Please I beg you, help me. I want to look across the water at it."

"Be dammed! She's gonna see!" says James, lifting me in his arms and carrying me to the railing. With my head nestled on his shoulder, I open my eyes. There in the distance appears a large sliver of land: America. My America. My new home. Too weak to look any longer, I close my eyes. Gently he puts me back down on the blanket where I can dream about my new home.

I hear Captain Anthony and Mr. Smith getting into a heated argument.

"I say we will, Mr. Smith!" the captain argues.

"We can't, Captain!" Samuel replies firmly. "It's near dark and too dangerous to port the ship. We're still half a day sailing until we reach port, which means we'd be pulling in in the middle of the night."

"I say we will, so make ready to port!" Captain Anthony demands. "She needs a doctor, and it's too far for the rowboats. We're going to port."

"We can't, Captain. We could ram the dock. We just can't!" Samuel says calmly.

I see the fight go out of the captain. "You're right," he admits. "But at first light I want this ship at full sail. We'll be heading into port. Hoist the distress flag. We'll ram any vessel that gets in our way."

"Aye, Captain," says Samuel.

36

As the ship pulls into port early the next morning, I hear a loud cannon firing a salute as our ship approaches the pier. Somehow word has gotten to them that we were headed to their port. I hear cheering crowds of townspeople who have gathered on the dock to see our arrival. Are they here to witness the return of the *Catalpa*?

The ship shakes as the chain drops the anchor, and I feel it slow to a stop. The *Catalpa* has arrived, and the crowd cheers even louder.

"Miss Adeleen, someone has gone to find a doctor for you," Peat tells me. "Jackson, pick up Miss Adeleen and take her to the rail so she can see her new home."

With tears running down my cheeks, I lock eyes with James as he smiles at me, giving me a slight wave. Then he and the other Irish walk down the footbridge and off the ship, with Mr. Breslin and Mr. Desmond following close behind. They must go because this is their celebration. The entire journey was for this moment.

I hear the loud cheers and joyous laughter from the crowd. But the Irish men's faces are solemn. I'm sure they can't believe it either, that they're free. Free from their hard living at the prison. How many have families here to welcome them? Probably none. But if they did, what would they think of them?

I know I'm not the same person either. I'm not a twelve-year-old girl anymore. We've been beaten, and suffered a great deal of the harsh treatment at the prison, but we all survived, and now we're in America.

The crowd cheers louder as all the Fenian men walk together onto American soil. Some of the returning prisoners have tears running down their faces as they smile and lift their hands to wave at the crowd. The people can't keep their hands off the rescued Irishmen, surrounding them and patting them on their backs. Little children wave American flags and cheer, while others are waving green flags for the Irish. They are free, and I'm free. What a jubilant welcome to my new home.

Exhausted, it's too much, and I can't watch anymore. I ask Jackson to put me back down on the deck so I can listen to the laughter coming from the pier. Closing my eyes, I dream. I too have overwhelming feelings. The desperation I have lived with for so long, along with the mental and physical hopelessness I endured, has ended. For the first time in years, I'm truly free. Falling asleep, I imagine seeing us in a new land far from our homelands of Ireland and England. We will start anew.

What will the men do now? Where will they go? Will I see any of them again? Who knows? Maybe they will board another ship to take them to their homeland. With that last conscious thought, I fall asleep.

Drifting in and out of sleep, I open my eyes. Looking up high to the mast that holds her furled sails, I know I never want to go on another ship again. Maybe they'll bury me somewhere under a blue tree. With millions of thoughts swirling in my head, I'm too tired to imagine any longer.

Across the deck the crew gathers at the rail to watch and wave to the welcoming crowd on the pier. Captain Anthony is a hero. He too stands with his crew at the rail waving to the crowd.

Their journey is over, and the ship has been made secure for its stay in port. It's time for the crew to head down the footbridge and off the ship. Some look back at me, waving. In my heart I want to thank them, but can only smile instead.

Occasionally the loud cannon fires again in celebration. Even though it hurts my ears, I think what a wondrous place this America must be. With all this excitement my mind lets go, and once again I lose sense of time.

I hear Samuel telling Captain Anthony they've had a hard time finding a doctor. So much time has passed since our arrival, the day is almost spent. The sun is starting to set. Fighting to stay conscious, I see Captain nervously standing on the ship's deck watching the cheering crowd as his crew of brave men disembark to join in the excitement. Why doesn't he go and join the celebration? Is something stopping him from leaving the ship? Could it be me?

James has gone to celebrate with the others. Captain has voyaged across the water for a year and a half. He has built up emotions that probably aren't so easily pushed aside. I know it is hard for me too. Will he ever sail again? Has it all been worth it?

He stands silently as a man and a lady climb the footbridge to board the ship. The man immediately comes over and talks to Peat. It's the doctor. He kneels down to examine me, then quickly gives me some medicine to drink. I'm grateful he's here. I look over and see the captain talking to the lady.

"Who is the lady?" I ask Peat. "She looks vaguely familiar."

"Oh, she's the Missus. She's Captain's wife."

"Jackson!" yells Peat. "Help carry Miss Adeleen to the doctor's buggy."

"Aye," says Jackson.

Lifting me in his arms, Jackson walks to the footbridge. I hold tight to my whale's tooth as we start down the bridge. I look over at the captain standing by his wife. He looks away to avoid eye contact with me, and my heart breaks.

It's the lady whose image was on the tin in the trunk. All this time he's had a wife waiting for him. I turn away in disgust, not wanting to look at them anymore. Too sick to try to understand, I take a deep breath, clutch my whale tooth, and bury my face on Jackson's chest, holding tightly onto him as he carries me down the footbridge and off the ship to America.

Waiting for me at the bottom of the bridge is James. He's come back.

"I'll take her," James says to Jackson and reaches out to carry me.

About the Author
Veatrice Chapin

Veatrice Chapin, known to friends as Veatie, was born and raised in Sacramento, California, and now resides in the nearby town of Roseville. With her English and Irish roots, she has always been drawn to stories about her heritage. Inspired by the remarkable true story of the *Catalpa* and the Fenians' 1876 legacy, she navigated through historical documents to write this fictionalized story.